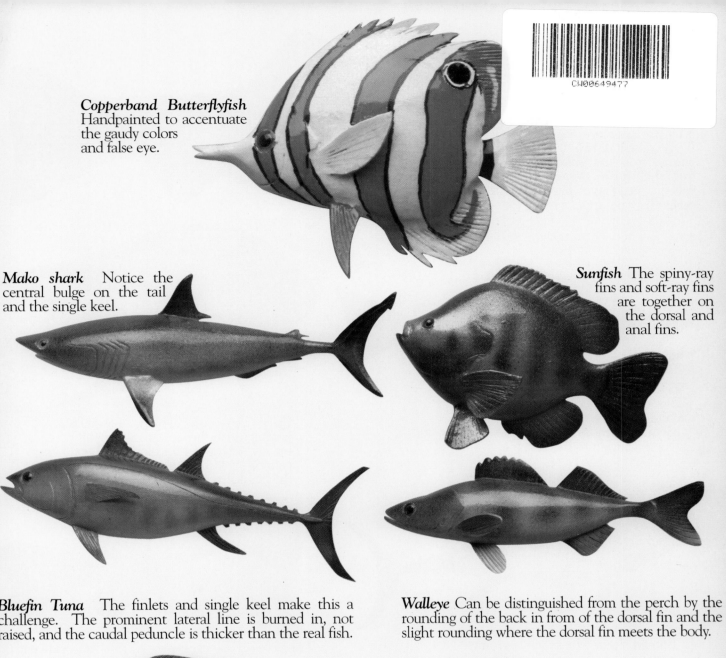

Copperband Butterflyfish
Handpainted to accentuate
the gaudy colors
and false eye.

Mako shark Notice the
central bulge on the tail
and the single keel.

Sunfish The spiny-ray
fins and soft-ray fins
are together on
the dorsal and
anal fins.

Bluefin Tuna The finlets and single keel make this a
challenge. The prominent lateral line is burned in, not
raised, and the caudal peduncle is thicker than the real fish.

Walleye Can be distinguished from the perch by the
rounding of the back in from of the dorsal fin and the
slight rounding where the dorsal fin meets the body.

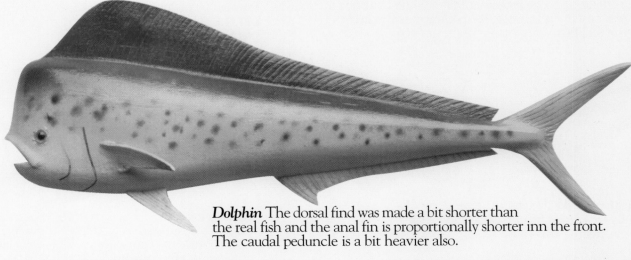

Dolphin The dorsal find was made a bit shorter than
the real fish and the anal fin is proportionally shorter inn the front.
The caudal peduncle is a bit heavier also.

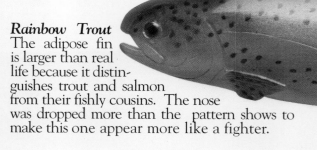

Rainbow Trout
The adipose fin is larger than real life because it distinguishes trout and salmon from their fishly cousins. The nose was dropped more than the pattern shows to make this one appear more like a fighter.

Sockeye Salmon
The deep hooks on the mandibles show this to be a spawning salmon, and teeth would be a good addition to this carving.

Queen Angelfish This is one of the hardest fish to do justice to as a minifish because of the color. Note the hand-painted gold highlights which hint at the highlights on the scales.

Bluefin Tuna The finlets and single keel make this a challenge. The prominent lateral line is burned in, not raised, and the caudal peduncle is thicker than the real fish.

Largemouth Black Bass Notice the open gills. The caudal peduncle was thickened for the tail flip, and the spiny dorsal fin reduced to heighten the effect of the open mouth and gills.

Northern Pike The teeth really make this fish. Notice the boxy effect of this fish.

Black Angelfish The gossamer effect of the fin cannot be captured in wood, but the white tipping helps portray its thin nature. The scale effect was done with a piece of bridal veil.

Sperm Whale This is an example of how the pattern can be developed into a full-body fish.

Sailfish This is one of the few fish that has the dorsal fin made separately and attached, because of its size. Note the hand-painted spots on the body.

Blue Marlin The bill was not superglued for strength and had to be repaired.

Black Crappie The dorsal and anal fins are good examples of soft-rayed and spiny-rayed fins. The black crappie makes a good pin or hat pin.

Carving Fish —
Miniature Saltwater and Freshwater

by James R. Jensen

Fox Chapel Publishing
Box 7948
Lancaster, PA 17604

Publisher: Alan Giagnocavo
Project Editor: Ayleen Stellhorn
Cover Design: Dennis Shirk
Cover Photography: VMI Productions, Leola, PA

ISBN # 1-56523-053-1

Carving Fish - Miniature Salt and Freshwater is a brand new work first published in 1995. The illustrations contained herein are copyrighted by James R. Jensen. Artists can make any number of projects based on these illustrations. The illustrations themselves, however, are not to be duplicated for resale or distribution under any circumstances. Any such action is a violation of copyright laws.

To order your copy of this book,
please send check or money order
for cover price plus $2.50 to:
Fox Chapel Book Orders
Box 7948
Lancaster, PA 17604-7948

Try your favorite book supplier first!

Acknowledgements

I hope that these patterns help fill the need for the top and front views needed to carve fish. Most pictures and photos of fish show the side view of the fish, but there are very few good top or front views. It is difficult to carve a realistic fish without having an idea of its basic shape.

My thanks to John Gresser for stirring my interest in fish carving and giving me many tips, especially on using the shadow box for displays. Thanks also to: Tim Hecht, of Hecht Taxidermy, for helping me with the painting of the fish and for his many tips and hints; Diana Jensen, for the typing and editorial help; and the carvers of the Blue Earth Royal Chislers and the Ceylon Carving Club, for their encouragement as I was writing the book. I also acknowledge Lori Peters, who helped with the initial photographing of the pictures and on many of the how-to pictures.

Table of Contents

Introduction

Fish carving is fun and easy to do, if you have a pattern and understand the few pitfalls that are easily avoided.

The objective of this book is to provide patterns and hints that will enable carvers to make mini fish of which they can be proud.

There are many good fish encyclopedias and fish guides available, but at best they only show a side view. These views are helpful for painting, but without a top view and a front view, they do not help carvers much. The patterns in this book show all three views.

Making patterns for carving mini fish requires some changes so that the fish does not get too fragile to carve. The patterns in this book are meant to be used on mini fish. If you intend to carve full-sized fish or enlarge these patterns over 200–300 percent, you should use other references along with these patterns to change the modified areas back.

If you reduce these patterns, you may have to modify certain areas more to keep the fish from becoming too fragile. This is usually not a problem and will not detract from the looks of your mini fish.

The mini fish shown in this book appear flat or with a minimum tail flip. The top and side views are shown as half-sections. Once you see the fish this way, it is easy to modify the pose. The fish all look good carved just like the pattern shows. You may want to try a few flat poses before you attempt to change poses.

On a full-bodied fish, you may want to thin the tail or body more than the half-section shows, but be careful to retain the correct body configuration for the fish you are carving.

The anatomical terms for the parts of a fish are kept to a minimum. Some parts cannot be described without using the correct anatomical terms. The terms used in this book are included on an illustration of a fish on page 58. This fish is not typical; it is meant to show the positions of the anatomical parts. Do not try to use this illustration as a pattern; you will have a very weird-looking fish.

Although whales and porpoises are mammals, for the purposes of this book they are included as fish. Be aware that flippers, fins, and flukes do not have rays; they are covered with flesh and are smooth.

The hints and suggestions given in this book are proven with both beginning and expert carvers, but they are by no means the only ways to get a finished carving. Try different methods of carving, as long as they are safe; you may find a better, faster, or easier method that is better suited to your style of carving. There are as many ways of carving as there are woodcarvers.

All of the information in this book applies to either hand carving or power-tool carving. One of the advantages of carving mini fish is that they can all be done with a bench knife (carving knife), which often can be purchased for less than $10.00. (Please do not use a jackknife. They tend to fold while carving, causing nasty cuts, and are usually a softer steel that requires more sharpening to maintain a good cutting edge.)

I hope that you will enjoy carving these fish and that you will get many compliments from your friends.

Carving
Step-by-Step

General Carving Tips

The tips and techniques in this book are proven with both beginning and expert carvers, but they are by no means the only ways to get to a finished carving. *There are as many ways of carving as there are woodcarvers.* Try different methods of carving, as long as they are safe. You may find a better, faster, or easier method that suits your style of carving.

Recommendations only	The steps in this book are recommended, especially for doing your first fish. Unless otherwise specified, the order is not critical and can be changed to suit your style of carving.
Strive to capture the "essence"	Remember that you can only capture the *essence* of the fish you are portraying. To paraphrase the poet, "Only God can make a fish." Your goal is to have your friends or customers recognize your carving as, for example, a Northern and not a muskie. The next time you go to the supermarket, check out the fish fillets and fish steaks for ideas on shape and other characteristics.
Wood selection	There are many good woods available for carving, but only a few are well-suited for mini fish. Basswood, yellow poplar, and tupelo are good, short-grained, moderately hard woods that will take the small detail of a mini fish without undue chipping or breaking. If you plan to paint your mini fish, use a plain wood like basswood or poplar. Butternut and walnut carve nicely and have beautiful grains, and it is a shame to cover them with paint. Woods like pine, fir, Philippine mahogany, and oak have a long, splintery grain and are better suited for construction projects or architectural work. The projects in this book were all carved from (northern) basswood, a wood that is readily available in most of the United States. Good basswood is becoming more expensive, but the price is still within the range of most carvers. If you are contemplating using other woods, experiment with scraps before you use the wood for your mini fish.

There are many ways to get your pattern onto the wood. You can make a template and trace the pattern. You can use graphite paper or carbon paper and trace the pattern onto the wood. Or you can use any number of the other methods described in carving books.

    The easiest, quickest, and least damaging to your pattern book is to photocopy the pattern. (You do not even have to remove it from the book.) Glue the photocopied pattern to the wood using rubber cement or spray adhesive. Apply the adhesive to the pattern only, so that the pattern can be easily removed. Saw cut to the outside of the line, and you are ready to start carving.

Keep your pattern in front of you while you are carving. Other reference material should be kept handy. You'll find that your confidence in your ability to carve that particular fish will increase faster if you have your pattern in front of you.

Unless you have carved a lot, you may find it easier to remove the majority of the material by blocking out (boasting out). Take the majority of wood off the fins and tail first. Then shape the body thickness using the top view as a guide. Finally, shape the body and head.

Once your fish is carved, an easy way to get ready for sanding is to use a 6" double-cut mill bastard file. A half-round file is handier than a flat file, but either one will work. A file will keep the surfaces of your fish flowing without dips or high spots and will not imbed grit into the wood.

During your sanding you may find that you want to carve more wood off of your fish. This is okay, but be aware that you'll need to strop your knife more often. Grit from sanding is abrasive to your knife edge and will cause your knife to dull faster.

If a part of your mini fish breaks off, *don't panic*. There is a simple way to repair your break. Do not sand, scrape, or clean the break in any way. Take both pieces and apply a bit of superglue

Transferring patterns

Reference material

Blocking out

Using a file

Carving during sanding

Fixing a break

(cyanoacrylic resin) to each piece at the break. In about 15–30 seconds the glue should have soaked into the wood; if not, quickly dab off any excess. Allow the superglue to set for 6–15 minutes until the parts are dry to the touch. Apply a drop of superglue and put the pieces together following the manufacturer's instructions. You now have a joint that can't be seen, but is stronger than the wood itself.

Strengthening fragile parts

Strengthen fragile parts of your fish, such as bills on sailfish, with superglue. Apply superglue and allow it to soak into the wood. If all the superglue has not soaked in by a minute or so, quickly dab off the excess. Now your fragile areas are no longer fragile. Superglue can be painted over with most paints.

No mistakes

There are no mistakes in woodcarving—unless you cut yourself. The best carvers in the world have to correct their work sometimes; that is why there are so many brands of wood putty. When you choose a wood putty, be sure to select one that will dry with a hardness close to the hardness of your wood. A careful selection will help to eliminate high or low spots when you're sanding.

Flat tails and tail flips

As you're following along with the steps in this book, you'll note several terms regarding the fish in the photos. The first two, flat tail and tail flip, as they suggest, refer to the position of the tail. Some photos show a fish carved with a tail that is flat, or in other words, follows along the same straight centerline as the head and body. Other photos show a fish with a slight curve to its tail, or a tail flip.

Half bodies and full bodies

You'll also see the words half-bodied and full-bodied. A half-bodied fish is a fish that's been split in half from head to tail along its centerline. The back of the fish is flat, making it easy to mount this type of carving directly on a plaque or wall. A full-bodied fish is one that has been carved in the round; both sides of the fish are finished. This type of carving is perfect for decorating desk sets, creating a diorama of a natural setting, or mounting on a decorative base.

Your friendly dentist has many tools which carvers can use; some he normally throws away when dull, others he may part with for a song. Carbide tips get dull for use on human teeth, but in conjunction with your power tools, they work nicely on wood. Probes, scrapers, and explorers that break or are sharpened too much for the dentist's use can be easily modified for carving.

Carving is only a matter of control of your tools and the wood. The more control you have, the better your carvings will be.

Carving the fin rays doesn't have to be difficult. In this book, the fin rays are shown as a single line so that you can see the spacing of the rays. On mini fish, these rays look good burned in as a single line, although on a real fish the fin rays are actually raised. If you want more realism, or if you're planning to carve a larger fish, you can burn or carve a double line for the actual ray and relieve the material between the lines with a very small gouge.

Fish fins are usually one of two types: spiny-rayed or soft-rayed. Usually, the first dorsal fin is spiny-rayed, and the other fins are usually soft-rayed. However, the first few rays on a soft-rayed fin may be spiny on some fish. The caudal fin, commonly known as the tail, is soft-rayed.

    Spiny-rays are stiff and pointed gradually to the tip. Soft-rays are flexible, not necessarily pointed, and may branch out. One of the best ways to picture soft-rays is to think of them as you would think of tree branches.

    The fish patterns in this book show the spiny-ray fins with a scalloped look; the soft-rayed fins are shown smooth.

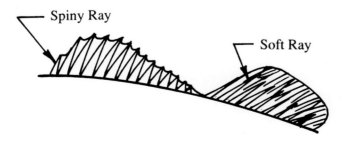

Spiny Ray

Soft Ray

Flippers, fins and flukes

Although whales and porpoises are mammals, for the purposes of this book they are included as fish. Be aware that flippers, fins, and flukes do not have rays; they are covered with flesh and are smooth.

Strengthening fins

Fins can be fragile and prone to breakage. One way to ensure that the fins on your fish won't break is to coat them with cyanoacrylic resin (superglue). Apply a generous coat to the carved and burned fin and allow it to soak into the wood for a minute or so. Quickly dab off any excess and let the fin dry. Your fragile fin is now probably stronger than the fish itself.

Plastic fins

Some carvers make fins out of thin plastic and attach them to the fish with auto body putty. This method may be more suitable for the larger fins, such as a sail on the sailfish, but it is really not suitable or necessary for most fish. Plastic is also harder to paint without proper preparation.

When you are carving fins that lay close to the body, such as pectoral fins, carve the back of the fin and detail it. Glue it to the body and then carve the front of the fin.

Fish eyes

Make sure you are using a fish eye and not a bird eye. Bird eyes are too round and make a fish look bug-eyed. Also, look for glass, and not plastic, eyes. When you are airbrushing a fish, the eye will become covered with paint. Acrylic- or lacquer-based paints will dissolve a plastic eye.

Superglue is safe to use if you follow a few simple precautions. First, read the manufacturer's instructions. Second, do not wash your hands immediately before using the superglue; the oil in your fingers will help keep the glue from bonding too tightly. If your fingers are too clean you can get a little oil by rubbing your earlobe or the side of your nose.

Enjoy carving your mini fish and take time out to admire your work as you carve.

Step One: Transferring and Sawing Out the Fish

Use a copy machine to make a photocopy of your pattern. In this demonstration, we're working with a Northern pike. Working with a copy ensures that you'll always have the original for reference and future use and is least damaging to your book.

Glue the side view onto your block of wood using rubber cement or spray adhesive. Apply the adhesive to the pattern only.

As you carve, keep your pattern in front of you. You'll find that having the pattern close at hand will save time and make you a more confident carver.

Remember as you scrollsaw or bandsaw to cut along the *outside* of the lines. Cutting directly on the lines or just to the inside of the lines may throw off your measurements. By following the outside of the lines, you'll have a little extra wood to play with. If you don't have a bandsaw or a scroll saw, a coping saw will also work.

There is no need to remove the pattern. Hold or glue the picture on your cutout and incise your stop cuts for the gills and fins. If you are using a glass eye, locate and drill the location for the eye hole; a $1/16$" diameter hole is big enough.

The small hole for the eye is seen in Step Four. The eye location hole can be drilled any time before the pattern is removed. It is best to drill it now before you forget it and have to do a lot of measuring to relocate it.

Step Two: Thinning the Fins

Carve the fins to $1/8''$ thick. This thickness will leave some wood for you to take off when you're finishing the fins and give enough strength to the fins to keep them from breaking while you carve the body. If you are carving a half-bodied fish, as shown in the photo, the fins will be located at the back of the body; on a full-bodied fish, the fins will be centered on the body.

Make a stop cut for the gill cover. Cut straight into the pattern and wood about $1/16''$ deep and make a chip cut on the waste side (body side) of the cut. This cut will keep your knife from cutting into or cutting off the gill cover when you are working on the body.

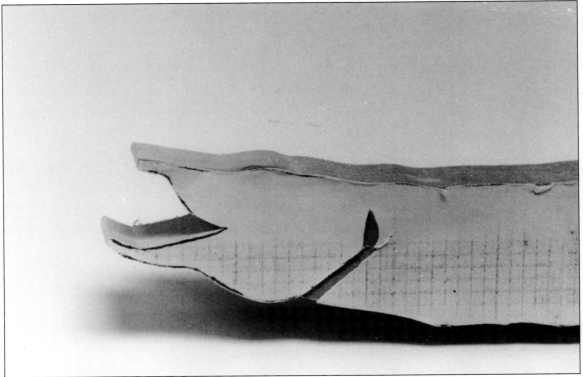

Step Three: Blocking Out

Blocking out is a technique that is useful for carvers to master. By using this technique, carvers will get a better feel for the overall shape of the fish and make the next step, rounding the body, easier.

To block out the fish, draw the top view onto the top of your cutout. Without making any attempt to round the edges or sides of your fish, remove any excess wood. Your objective is to take the fish's body down to its correct thickness.

Note that at this stage the head is left alone and still has the paper pattern attached to it. The line of the gill cover has been extended up to the top of the back to allow the full length of the body to be carved. At this point, don't worry too much about the smoothness of the body.

If you are carving your fish with a tail flip, draw the general shape you desire on the top of your cutout. Remove the material in back of the tail to the general shape, then thin the front of the tail to approximately 1/8" thick. If you are working on a flat-tailed pose, thin the tail to approximately 1/8" thick.

Step Four: Shaping the Body and the Tail

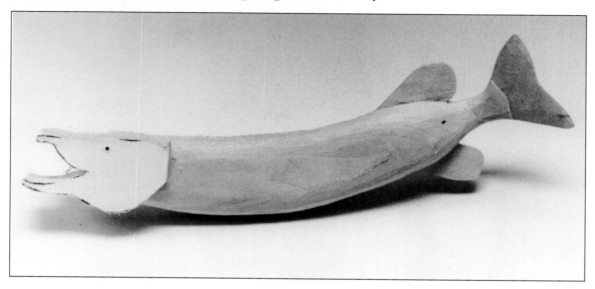

With the body of the fish blocked out, visualizing the finished body shape is now a simple task. It's easy to see how to round the sides and edges to get those smooth, flowing lines. The front view of the fish shows the fish at its widest point (usually its middle) and will help you to shape the fish from the front.

As you carve the fish to its final shape, also carve the fins and the tail down to their final thickness. You will probably not want to get the fins thinner than 1/32"; 3/64" is a good thickness on basswood. Remember you may want to burn in the fin rays. Note that on a real fish, there is not a sharp corner where the fins join the fish's body. This bit of realism is hard to attain on a mini fish, and you may opt to leave the inside corners sharp.

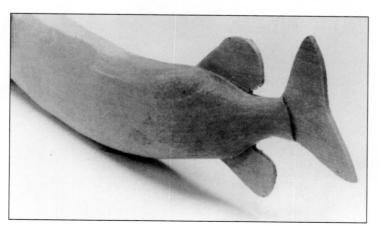

The caudal peduncle (the area just in front of the tail) is thicker than the tail. To get a more realistic-looking fish, do not blend the area where the tail fin joins the body. Leave the caudal peduncle slightly raised about 1/64", but rounded on the top.

Step Five: Shape the Head

Now that your mini fish has the proper body shape, you can start carving the head. Using the pattern as a guide, draw the top view of the head on your fish. Block out the head. The head shape on most fish (and all the ones in this pattern book) blends into the body. The mandibles protrude on some fish, and on others, they are a virtual continuation of the head. The upper mandible overlaps the lower and, at the hinge joint, does protrude from the opercle. If you are carving your fish with open gills, remember that on most fish the outside of the gills is stiff and moves like a cover plate. Gill covers (opercle) do not dish out. You may find it easier to carve the rest of the head before carving the gill cover on open-gilled fish.

When you have the head fully shaped, relieve the inside of the mouth from the back so that you cannot see the wood inside when you look at the fish from the side. Approximately $1/16"$ of relief is usually enough. Mini fish do not require mouth detailing.

Step Six: Sanding

After you have carved your mini fish, an easy way to get ready for sanding is to use a 6" double-cut mill bastard file (sometimes called a 6" mill file). A half-round file is handier than a flat file, but either one will work. A file will keep the surfaces of your fish flowing without dips or high spots and will not imbed grit into the wood. Other files that may come in handy are automobile point files or Swiss or American pattern needle files (either #0 or #2 cut).

Sand the fish smooth. The smoother you can get the fish the better it will look when you apply the finish. Most fish look best wet and slick and slippery.

Small details, unless they help to identify the fish, can be left off. You also may find that it is easier to woodburn the smaller details.

Note the scooped out area under the gill. The pectoral fin will be inserted here later. (See "Step Nine" for more details about how to carve this area.)

Step Seven: Add the Teeth

You'll only need the information in this step if you are carving a fish with the teeth showing. Northern pike, muskies, salmon, and piranhas all look good with an open mouth and teeth. Use only enough teeth to give a "toothy" look. Don't try to duplicate nature.

To make the teeth, use a scissors to cut a strip $3/16"$ wide from an aluminum can. Cut teeth-shaped wedges from the strip. When you are ready to insert the teeth (not before), cut a slit approximately $1/16"$ - $3/32"$ deep in the jaw. A needlenose pliers works well to insert the teeth. Glue isn't necessary because the wood will tighten up on the aluminum teeth.

Cut the teeth from a $3/16"$-wide strip of aluminum.

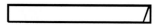

Step Eight: Place the Eye

If you are using a glass eye, you have drilled a small eye hole location. Enlarge the eye pocket a little larger ($1/64''$ to $1/32''$ larger) than the eye you are going to use. One of the easiest ways to make an eye pocket is to use a drill bit of the proper size, hold it in your fingers, and turn it back and forth to get the proper depth. The eye pocket should be deeper than the final depth of the eye to allow room for the epoxy or whatever you are going to use to mount the eye.

Ribbon epoxy (yellow/blue), Kulis Karvit™, or tan plumbers putty (not grey—it has metal fill) works well for setting eyes. The thick, two-part, slower-setting epoxies work much better than the fast epoxies. Glaziers putty is too oily for fish carvings. The oils bleed into the wood, keeping the putty from getting hard.

Mount the eye and remove and smooth any excess material that oozed past the eye. Dental tools work well for this task. If the epoxy builds up on your tool, wipe it off with your fingers. The natural oil on your fingers should keep the epoxy from sticking.

Once the eye is set there is no need to move it. If you use plumbers putty, make sure that you paint it with gesso because acrylics attack it, causing the putty to break down.

Note: A fish eye is aspherical. Place it so the point of the pupil is toward the front.

Step Nine: Attaching the Fins

Do any detailing on the fish, such as gills, back of fins, and scales, now before you attach the fins to the body.

Several fins on your fish may need to be carved as inserts. Using the patterns, cut these fins from a 3/32"- to 1/8"-thick piece of wood. Many hobby stores carry a thin basswood called microwood that works well for inserted fins. Carve the pectoral fin, pelvic fin, and other fins with a slight convex shape to the back. Burn or carve the details of the rays on the back of the fins only.

Scoop out a pocket on the body of the fish to accept the fin. In this photo, you can see an example of a scooped-out area where the pectoral fin will go. The pocket should be V-shaped and not quite as deep as your rough-shaped fins. Fins look best when placed at a 10°–30° angle from the body. Any angle within this 10°–30° range will look fine. Glue the fins in place.

Shape the front of the fins. A simple concave cup shape on the outside of the fin is enough to show some action and realism.

In this photo, the pelvic fin has been shaped and attached to the body.

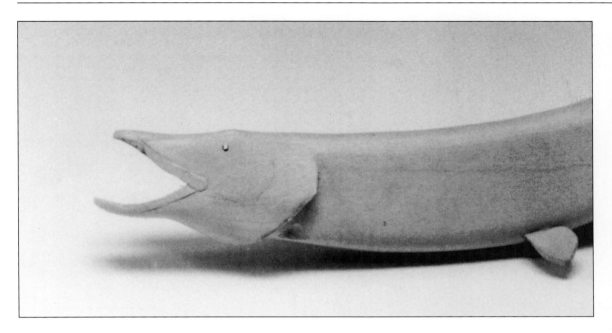

Step Ten: Burn the Fins

The fin rays on the patterns are a single line so that you can see the spacing of the rays.

The first dorsal fin is spiny-rayed so the rays are stiff and pointed gradually to the tip. These rays look good burned in as a single line, although on a real fish the fin rays are actually raised. You can burn or carve both sides of the ray and relieve the material between the rays with a very small gouge if more realism is desired.

The other fins and the tail (caudal fin) are soft-rayed. Soft rays are flexible and branch out, somewhat like the branches on a tree. Burn the single lines (the tree trunks) from the bottom to the top of the fin first and then fill in the branches.

Your fish is now finish carved and, except for painting and mounting, it is a work of art. Take some time and admire your work; you are entitled to say this is a job well done.

Jim says...

"A sharp tool cuts wood; a dull tool cuts fingers."

"If you feel that you are going to cut yourself, you will."

"The only mistake in woodcarving is cutting yourself."

Painting
Step-by-Step

General Painting Tips

Now that your fish is nicely carved, you want your fish to look as realistic as you can make it. This is where painting comes in. Anyone can learn to paint, but if all this painting seems beyond your capacities, do not despair. You may find that your taxidermist friend will do your fish painting at a nominal cost. *This is not cheating.* Many fine carvers can not paint (maybe that's why they are such good carvers) and have others do their painting.

In the following photos, Tim Hecht, master taxidermist, professional fish carver, and friend, uses lacquer-based paints and an airbrush to paint a Northern pike. The same results can be achieved with acrylic paints.

Natural finishes

Before we go any further, you may want to let the natural beauty of the wood show through, especially if your fish is stylized. Many carvers just seal or finish their fish, and their work looks wonderful, so you might want to try it. If you do choose not to paint (or stain), you should seal the carving all around (including the back) to prevent it from absorbing humidity and protect it from fingerprints and dirt. Fish tend to look dull and lifeless quickly as they accumulate dust and dirt.

Reference material

Because fish colors change right away after the fish is out of the water, a good color picture book is necessary. There are many good fish guidebooks available with either artistic renderings or photographs that you can use to paint your fish. Don't overlook outdoor magazines for photos either. If you can interpret and adjust for shade, the time the photo was taken, and exposure that the picture was taken under, the photo picture books may suit your purposes. Most people can work better with artists' pictures rather than photographs. One advantage or disadvantage that artists' pictures give you is that they are true for the species at the best time in the fish's life, ie: mating colors, adult stage, etc.

Airbrushing and hand-brushing

Airbrushing your fish is recommended, because of the blending of colors, but don't disregard hand-brushing completely.

There are many fish hand-brushed in oils that are beautiful. Many of the fish painting colors are premixed for use in an air-brush, but they can be used with a hand brush, also.

If your fish does not have scales, gesso applied to your fish and sanded makes a smooth base coat for your finish coats. If your fish has scales burned on, seal your fish with a good, non-water based sealer without fillers. A good way to tell if it is a non-waterbased sealer is to read the label. If the instructions on the can require clean-up with mineral spirits, naptha, or paint thinner, the gesso is non-waterbased.

You may burn after applying gesso, but do not burn over sealers. The fumes are terrible and breathing in too many of them can be deadly.

Painting is not just daubing some colors on your fish and hoping some miracle will make it look okay. You must know your paints and finishes, or you will end up with a botched job that will take longer to correct than doing it right the first time. Some common paints and their advantages and disadvantages follow:

Acrylics

Advantages: Fast-drying; water-soluble; many colors; no smell; easy clean-up.

Disadvantages: Fast drying makes blending difficult; can look unnatural.

Oils

Advantages: Slow-drying for easy blending; many colors; easy mixing.

Disadvantages: Slow-drying; some smell; clean-up requires solvents.

Alkyds

Advantages: Medium drying time for blending; low smell; easy clean up.

Disadvantages: Limited availability in some areas.

Lacquers

Advantages: Fast-drying; has shine built in; levels nicely when air-brushed; hard finish.

Gesso

Comparing paints

Disadvantages: Strong smell; requires patent solvents; clean-up requires solvents; requires ventilation because of flammability and toxicity; may not be readily available.

There are good paints in both acrylic and lacquer on the market, developed with the colors required by fish painters. (Lifetone and Polytranspar are just two of the manufacturers.) Your local taxidermist may supply your needs also, as it does not take much paint to do a mini fish.

Hiding flaws

Airbrushing with lacquer-based paints will not help to hide flaws in your carving—just the opposite happens. Once you've finished painting your fish, you can't go back and sand some more. Be sure that the surface of your fish is smooth before you begin to paint. Some common flaws that you should be on the lookout for include scratches from sanding, ripples (high and low spots) from sanding or from the wood grain, incomplete fills or rough spots from the wood putty used, fingernail marks or dents, glue lines, and unwanted knife marks.

Fish eyes

When using an airbrush to paint a fish, you'll end up covering the fish's eye with paint. Because of this, you'll want to use a glass fish eye instead of a plastic eye. Plastic eyes will dissolve with the application of lacquer- or acrylic-based paints. Also, make sure you're using a fish eye and not a bird eye. Bird eyes are too round overall, and the pupil is also round. The end result of a fish with bird eyes will be a bug-eyed fish.

Finishing touches

Your fish will still look flat when it is finish-painted. Get a good clear glazing lacquer and apply one or two (or more) coats to get that wet and slippery look.

When your fish is finished, proudly sign and date it. Some carvers number their work also, but this is up to you.

Step One:
Prepare the
Surface

Prime the fish with a thin coat of gesso. The gesso should be thinned approximately 50 percent with water or follow the manufacturer's instructions. Note: Some manufacturers recommend Matte Medium and water, but the Matte Medium does not seem necessary for wood.

Once the gesso is dry, sand the fish with 220-grit sandpaper. You can finish-sand with 320-grit for that ultra showroom smoothness, if you like. The gesso is sanded to achieve a smooth surface under the paint.

Step Two:
Apply Bronze
Color

Spray bronze on the upper two-thirds of the body and lightly on the fins. Spray from the top of the fish down so that the paint lightens in coverage as you approach the belly. On a small fish there is not a lot of room for blending, but without blending, the fish would look bland.

**Step Three:
Apply Olive
Green Color**

Apply olive green to the back, fins, and top of the head. Coat the back and the top of the opercle with the heaviest application of paint. The sides show the blending of the green and the bronze, which really gives the fish its Northern pike "look." If you stopped painting now, there would be no mistaking this fish as a Northern or muskie.

**Step Four:
Add the
Fighting
Blush**

Use gill red, a blood-red color, to create the fighting blush on the fins and under the gill cover. The red at this stage appears gaudy now, but the next stage will tone it down. If you want less blush, use thinner paint and a faster stroke to achieve a lighter coating. If you are doing fish for fishermen, they expect to see this fighting blush.

**Step Five:
Add Black**

Lightly spray black on the back and on the upper and lower mandible. Spray black spots on the fins and tail. The black on the fins and tail tends to tone down the red quite a bit.

**Step Six:
Add White**

Putting spots, stripes, or markings on the side of a fish is the hardest part of painting a mini fish. The markings on this fish have been sprayed on with the airbrush. The markings can also be hand-brushed. A combination of hand- and spray-brushing has also been tried with varying degrees of success. You may want to experiment with various techniques to see which effect you think looks best.

Step Seven: Clean the Eye

The fish is now finish-painted and the paint has been scraped off the eye with a knife, fingernail, dental pick, or any other suitable tool. This step shows the importance of using a glass fish eye, instead of a plastic eye or bird eye. Bird eyes are too round, and the pupil is round also, making the fish look bug-eyed.

Step Eight: Touch-up the Mouth

This photo shows the touch-up done with white paint inside the mouth. Apply the white lightly so that the inside of the mouth doesn't appear to be a stark white. This photo also shows the subtleties of the color blends on the side and the back of the fish.

Now is not the time to try for a matte finish. Apply as many coats of clear lacquer as you need to get that shiny, "fishy" look. As the coating ages, it seems to lose some of its high luster and look more natural. Apply the lacquer with a spray can or an airbrush. Follow the manufacturers directions, especially if using a spray can.

After all the work you've put into painting your mini-fish, it is time to sit back and admire your work.

Step Nine:
Apply a Clear,
Shiny Finish

Burning Scales
Step-by-Step

General Burning Tips

Although burning scales is not recommended on mini fish, it can be effective on larger fish. The crappie that is shown here has been enlarged 154 percent. The thickness and depth of the burn is exaggerated for photographing and would not be this pronounced for a fish of this size.

Also note that because pencil marks do not show up well in photographs, a marking pen was used to sketch in guidelines. This practice is *not* recommended. Wood has a tendency to absorb ink. You may find it difficult to remove the marks, and they bleed through gesso like crazy. Use a pencil whenever you need to make marks on the wood.

Less is more	Follow this general rule when you are burning to add realism and detail to your mini fish. The bigger the fish, the more detail it will bear; the smaller the fish, the less detail.
Reference material	Be sure to visit your nearest aquarium store or bait-and-tackle shop before you begin to layout the scales on your fish. Look closely at the minnows or guppies to get an idea of just how small and thin the scales are on small fish. In this chapter, you'll learn how to layout and burn scales on your carved fish. You will not be able to make your scales as thin as those on a real fish, but you must strive to keep the scales as thin as possible.
Etching scales	There are two methods of depicting scales, etching and burning. While etching the scales into the wood is easier than burning, it does have two drawbacks. First, if you are using a soft wood, you must seal the fish before starting or many of your etched marks will pop back out when you paint (especially if you are using water-based acrylics). Second, because you'll be using a drafting pencil or a sharp metal stylus to etch the scales, controlling the depth of the etch marks is difficult.
Tools for etching	If you do decide to etch scales, use a 6H or (preferably) a 9H drafting pencil or a sharp metal stylus to lightly engrave the scales on the fish. A broken dental tool, such as a probe or explorer, can be refashioned to make a long-lasting stylus.

Burning in the scales is the method demonstrated here. The burning tool makes clean, permanent marks, and it is much easier to control the depth of each mark.

Burning scales

The woodburner is a moderate-cost item, but it can be used for other woodcarving projects as well. A wire-type woodburner with a good heat control works best for burning scales. Some manufacturers now have fish-burning tips available that you may want to try. Once you learn to control the size of the scales with these tips, they may suit your needs. Attempting to burn scales with an element-type burner is extremely difficult. A wire-type burner is highly recommended for heat control. It is also cooler in your hand, which becomes important after a couple hours of burning.

Tools for burning

Burning scales (or etching them if you are opting for that method) will be easier if you leave the pectoral and pelvic fins off until after the scales have been burned. These fins will hinder the movement of the burner and may break as you attempt to work around them.

Attach fins later

When burning, the tip does the work, not you. Experiment with the heat setting until you find the best setting for your desired effect. As you get faster on your strokes, you may have to increase the heat to compensate.

Let the burner do the work

If your hand gets tired or cramped, you are pushing the burner into the wood rather than letting the burner burn the wood, as it was designed to do.

Scale-Burning Sequence

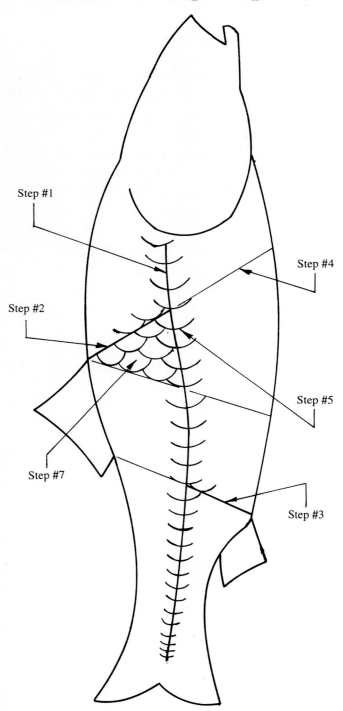

Step #1

Step #4

Step #2

Step #5

Step #7

Step #3

Step One: Layout the Scales

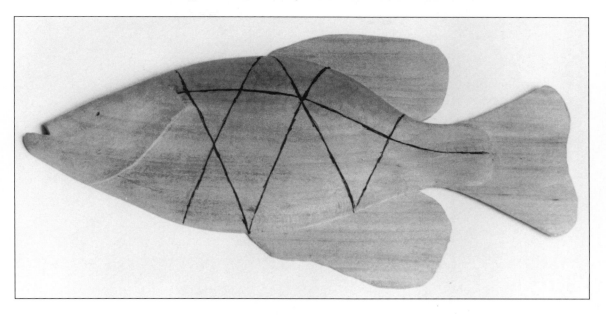

Lightly draw on the lateral line with a soft #2 or #2B pencil. This lateral line follows the backbone (spine) of the fish and is usually the thickest part of the fish's cross-section. On your next visit to the supermarket, look at the fish fillets to see where it is. Some fish have a more distinct lateral line than others.

Draw in your first diagonal line above the lateral line at approximately a 60° angle from directly in front of the dorsal fin to the lateral line. Extend this line below the lateral line.

Draw in a second diagonal line below the lateral line at approximately a 60° angle from directly in front of the anal fin to the lateral line. Extend this line above the lateral line.

Draw in the remainder of the diagonal lines as shown in the photograph. These lines will divide the fish into sections for burning.

Note: Using a marking pen is not recommended because the ink may make permanent marks in the wood. It was used here for photographic purposes only.

Step Two: Draw Scales on the Lateral Lines

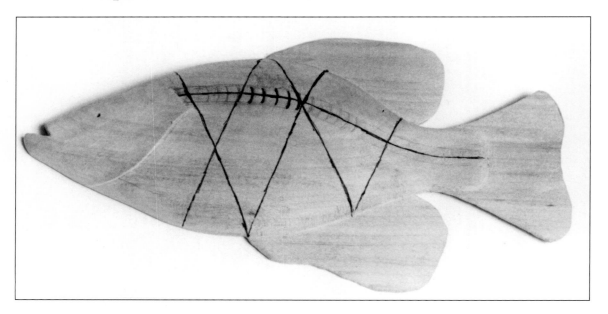

At the widest part of the fish, sketch in the first scale along the lateral line. This will be the largest scale on the fish. Notice that I've used a pencil to lightly draw in the remaining scales along the lateral line. This step is not necessary, but it may help you to visualize the decreasing size of the scales.

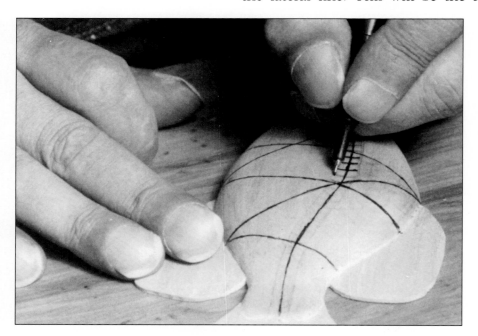

Step Three: Draw in the Diagonal Lines

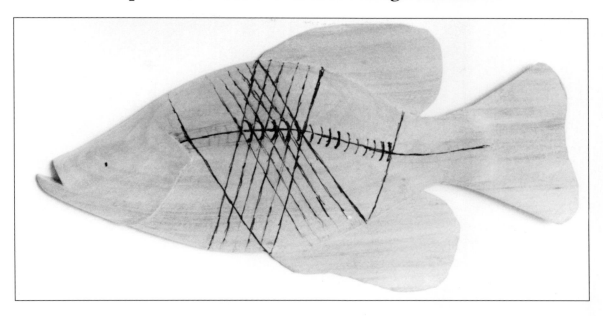

Lightly divide the fish into diamonds by drawing in lines parallel to the lines you drew in Step One. The size of the diamonds should decrease in size from the largest scale to the head and then from the largest scale to the tail. For this demonstration, I've drawn in only enough lines to fill the first triangular section.

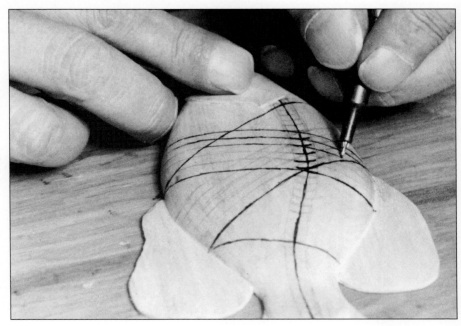

Step Four: Draw in the Scales

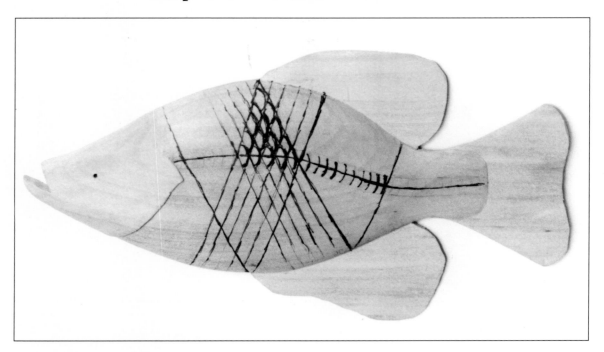

Start filling in your diamonds with lightly sketched-in scales. The pattern of the scales should be an even gradation from large in the middle to gradually decreasing both ways to the head and tail. As you do each diamond, try to have the scale meet the line. If the scales do not meet the line, either adjust accordingly or move the line.

Step Five: Burn in the Scales

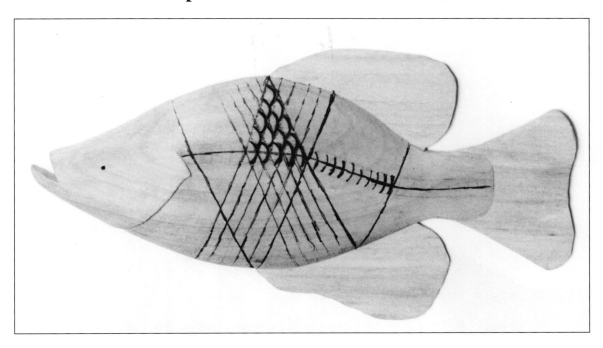

Burn in the scales. Experiment with the heat setting until you find the desired effect. Remember that the burn marks in these photographs are slightly exaggerated so they show clearly in the photographs.

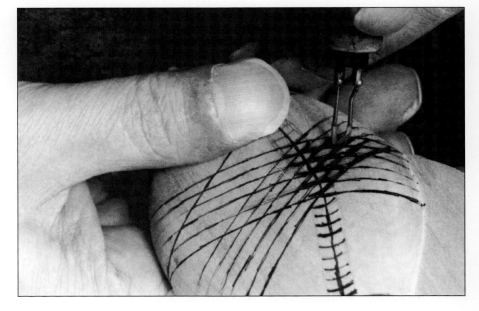

Step Six: Continue Burning Scales

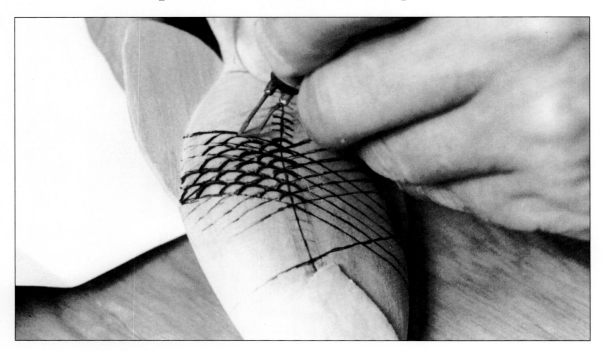

When burning, the tip of the woodburner does the work, not you. If you find that your hand is getting tired as you burn, you are pushing the burner into the wood rather than letting the burner burn the wood.

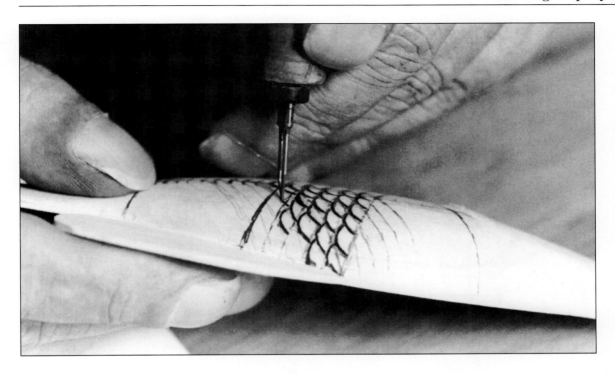

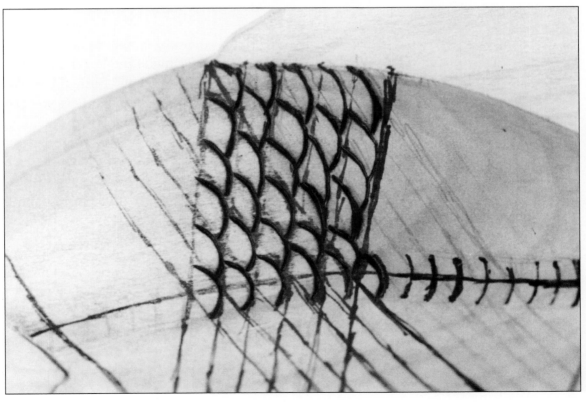

Step Seven: Burn in the Belly Scales

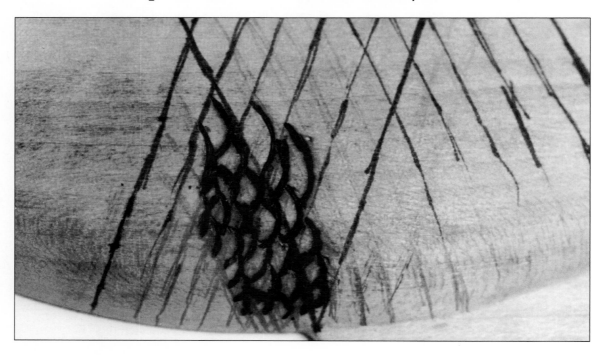

The belly scales on a fish are somewhat smaller than the fish's other scales. To draw these scales, divide the larger diamonds in half. Burn the scales here as lightly as you can and yet still be able to see them. Here again, the belly scales were burned darker than normal for photographic purposes.

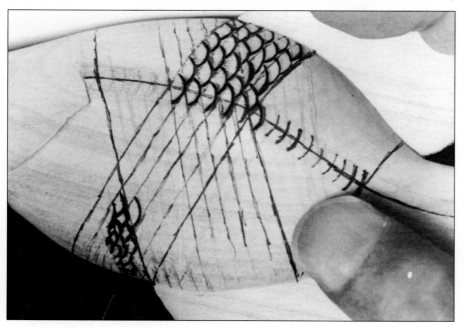

Step Eight: Finish Burning the Scales

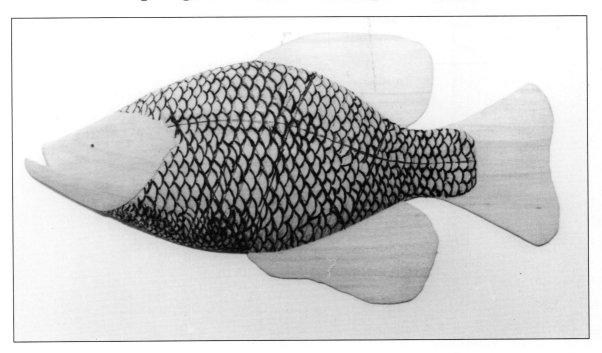

Once you've finished burning in the scales, use a medium tooth-brush to remove any charred wood from the fish. Charred wood does not take paint well and must be removed before you can begin to paint.

Your fish is ready for finishing, but with all the time you devoted to adding the scales, it is time to admire your work and give yourself a pat on the back.

Jim says...

*"There are as many ways of carving wood
as there are woodcarvers."*

*"There is no such thing as a bad carving;
be proud of your work."*

Displaying Mini Fish

Displaying Mini Fish

There are many ways to display and use mini fish. The suggestions given here may trigger other useful and novel ways that haven't been tried before or are just fun to do.

One of the ways to show your mini fish is to use a deep picture frame. (See pattern of picture frame on page 52.) This type of display keeps your carving behind glass and eliminates dusting and cleaning, which tends to deteriorate the finish. (For this reason, deep picture frames are popular with house wives, house husbands, and anyone else who hates to dust.) Some people paint scenes on the mounting board or use aquarium photos. One even mounted his Northern vertically and put a snapshot of himself next to the fish.

Sportsmen can have a memento of their lunker catch on an office wall without taking up a lot of space. Possibly a small brass plaque with the size and weight and day caught could be incorporated in the frame to bring back fond memories and document the bragging rights.

Mount a leaping mini fish on a desk set for an interesting way to organize pens and pencils.

A leaping fish mounted on a desk set makes a dramatic gift for the person who has everything. People who do not fish and/or belong to environmental clubs may wish to make a statement on the ecology, especially on endangered species, and what better way than with a wood carving.

There are many fishing clubs that award special trophies or plaques and are always looking for appropriate prizes. They may want to use your half-bodied fish on a plaque or a full-bodied fish on a trophy at their next outing.

A simple wood base shows off your full-bodied mini fish nicely and make a perfect mantelpiece display or tasteful knick-knack shelf item.

A half-bodied fish with a pin clasp on the back would make a neat pin for a cap or sweater to show your interest in fishing. Some clubs may want one for every member.

A single Northern or marlin with a lure or fly, leaping for the sky and trying to shake the hook, is sure to get the fisherman's juices flowing. Any fish posed in a natural setting will interest even the most casual observer.

A diorama of two or three mini fish does not require the amount of space that a full-size fish diorama would take and is a perfect conversation piece in a small apartment or a large living room.

If your full-bodied fish is sealed well with a few waterproof gloss coats, you may want to have it in the bottom of your aquarium with the tropical fish. Imagine a small whale or shark in with your tropical fish.

As you can see, there is a multitude of ways you can show off your creations, and your imagination can come up with many more.

Making a Picture Frame

Make your picture frame out of any kind of wood. Pine that has been wire-brushed to raise the grain and stained a greyish-white is attractive, natural-looking, and nicely sets off most of the mini fish in this book. Walnut or oak frames make a nice formal setting for your mini fish.

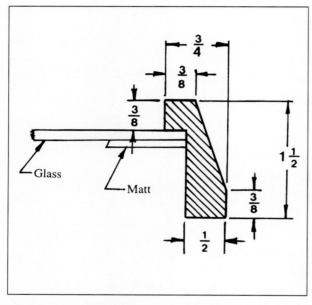

This cross-section shows how to make a neat, professional-looking frame.

Three sizes of frames work nicely for all of the fish in this book. Their outside dimensions are 6" x 8", 6" x 9" and 6" x 11$\frac{1}{2}$".

The depth of the frame should fit the fish being displayed plus $\frac{1}{8}$"–$\frac{1}{4}$" extra. Setting your fish too deep in the frame hides it. Usually a 1" depth is sufficient, but you'll want to measure your mini fish carefully.

Use a matt to help set off your mini fish and hide the inside of the frame. If you finish the inside of your frame, you may want to omit the mat. You can also insert a picture as a background for your fish.

Pattern
Section

General Pattern Tips

In carving, understanding how to use a pattern is just as important as knowing how to use a carving knife or a woodburner. Without learning the basics, your carving could be off to a flawed start right from the beginning. So, with that in mind, take some time to review the mini-fish patterns in this book before you start to carve.

Anatomically altered patterns

The fish in these patterns have been altered anatomically to make carving at such a small size easier. If you compare these fish to an actual fish, you'll note that the fins on the mini fish are thicker and sometimes larger in proportion than the actual fish. While these changes are slight and do not detract from the overall appearance of the species, they are necessary. Without them, certain areas on the fish, such as fins and tails would become too fragile to carve.

If you plan to reduce these patterns to an even smaller size, say to create a pin, you'll want to alter your pattern more. Make the fins longer and thicker and the body stockier to keep your fish from breaking as you carve.

If you plan to enlarge these patterns, the reverse is true. You'll need to shorten fins and thin out the fish. When enlarging these patterns more than 200–300 percent, be sure to compare the details carefully to other fish photos and reference materials and make any necessary adjustments before you begin to carve.

Flat poses

The fish patterns in this book are all based on a flat pose or tail flip—no leaps, no bends. If this is your first venture into miniature fish carving, try carving several fish in their flat, no-action poses before attempting to carve an "active" fish. If you're well-versed in fish carving, see the tips on modifying patterns on pages 56 and 57. These tips will help you to alter your fish's pose to create a more action-packed version of the fish you want to carve.

You can use these patterns to carve either a full-bodied fish or a half-bodied fish. The top and side view patterns are shown as half-sections, so if you are carving a half-bodied fish, you'll want to use them as is.

     If you are carving a whole fish, you may want to see the top and front as a whole body. The easiest way to make the whole body is to have a copy made on overhead transparency film. (This is a clear film.) Turn the film copy over and tape it to your original at the centerline. Then recopy the original and the transparency on plain paper, and you have a pattern for a full-bodied fish.

The front view of the fish patterns shows the fish at its thickest part. Fish are usually quite streamlined to enable them to catch food or escape enemies.

Half- or full-bodied

Using the front view

Modifying Patterns

Once you have carved a few mini fish flat or with a tail flip you may want to get more action in your mini-fish poses. Or you may want to stylize your fish, such as was done on the last pattern of a stylized porpoise.

There is nothing wrong with modifying the patterns to suit your taste: a longer fin, a fatter body, a more open mouth, or whatever is desired. Fish, like people, come in different sizes and shapes. As long as your fish looks like the species it is meant to represent, it is good.

Modifying a fish pattern is easy, if a few simple guidelines are followed.

Know the fish's anatomy

Not knowing the fish's anatomy can lead to unnatural poses. The following four tips address the biggest faults that will make a fish look unrealistic and that many carvers miss on their fish carvings.

Most fish use their tails (caudal fin) and caudal peduncle for propelling themselves through the water, so this is the most flexible part of the fish's body. This area is where you are going to see the most movement on your action fish.

The rib cage of the fish cannot bend much (like your rib cage.) Probably the biggest mistake carvers make is making the fish flex too much in the rib area and getting an unnatural looking fish. The rib area is roughly from the head to the anal fin. A flat-bodied fish can not bend across the flat area.

The pectoral and pelvic fins are used for steering and balance. These fins can move in almost any direction and can be cupped or flat. These fins can give a fish character and charm in the way you set them.

The fish's mouth hinges at the joint of the mandibles, but there is a fleshy connection between the mandibles which allows the fish to open its mouth larger than a simple pivot joint would. When carving a fish with an open mouth, the bottom of the jaw seems to extend in a smooth curve to the outer gill cover (opercle).

Keep the lateral line correct

In order to modify your fish you want to keep your fish the right length. There is only one measurement you have to make to keep the length of your fish in the proper proportion and that is the lateral line measurement.

The easiest way to lay out a fish with a simple curve is to saw your block to the rough configuration you want, looking from the top of your fish. Don't try to cut the final shape on the curve, but allow extra material so that the final shape can be adjusted to the curve. Glue the pattern to the side of the block and cut your fish out. The following sketches will show you how simple it is to get an action pose.

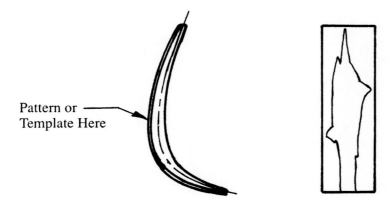

Pattern or Template Here

To stylize fish, you must determine which points or areas you want to stress and what can be left off and still get a fish that depicts the type of fish you have in mind.

On the stylized porpoise pattern shown on page 84, the eyes and the blowhole were left off and the belly was flattened to emphasize the flowing lines of the porpoise. The body was lengthened to make the lines flow. As can be seen from the stylized porpoise, there are really no rules for stylizing mini fish. Your knowledge and experience and what you want to show are the only criteria that count when stylizing fish. Stylizing fish is a good way to do your own thing.

Adding a curve

Stylized fish

Anatomy of a Fish

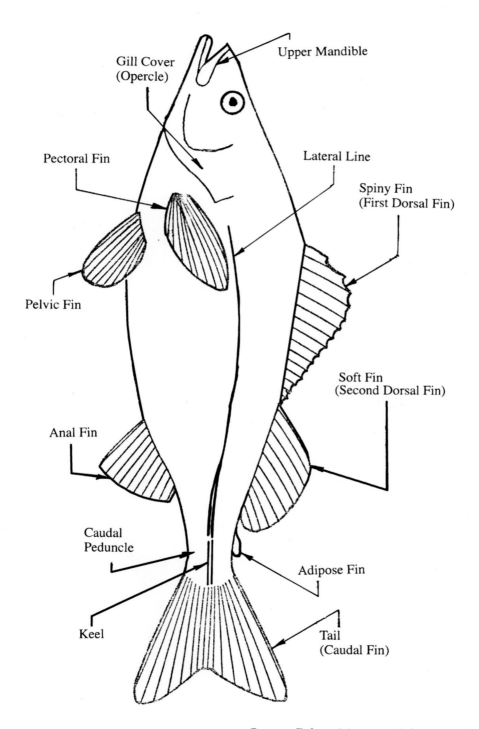

Gill Cover
(Opercle)

Upper Mandible

Pectoral Fin

Lateral Line

Spiny Fin
(First Dorsal Fin)

Pelvic Fin

Soft Fin
(Second Dorsal Fin)

Anal Fin

Caudal
Peduncle

Adipose Fin

Keel

Tail
(Caudal Fin)

Carving Fish — Miniature Saltwater and Freshwater

SPERM WHALE
(Physeter macrocephalus)

Body Color: Brownish grey back and sides. White around the mouth

The sperm whale was a highly prized catch both for its blubber and spermacetti (used in perfume).

The sperm whale has been a model for many carvings and was used for signs, weather vanes, etc., and is a fun fish (mammal) to carve either smooth or with the wrinkles from the flipper to the flukes.

Poses: Sperm whales look good fully carved and used on a base or desk set.

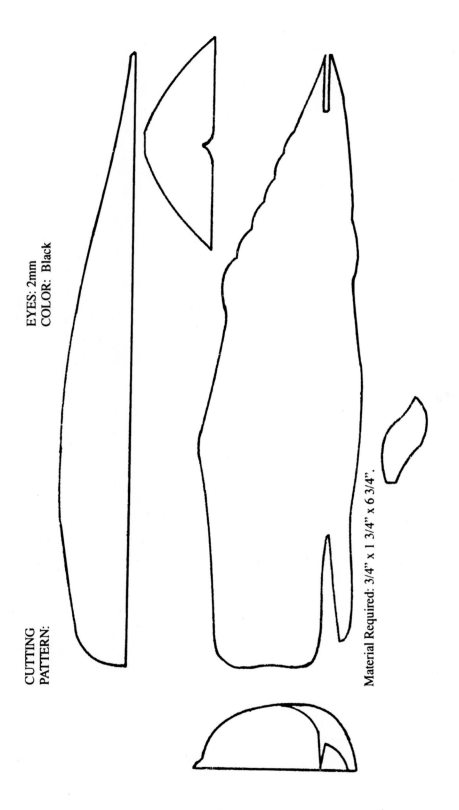

EYES: 2mm
COLOR: Black

CUTTING
PATTERN:

Material Required: 3/4" x 1 3/4" x 6 3/4".

BOTTLENOSED PORPOISE or DOLPHIN
(Tursiops truncatus)

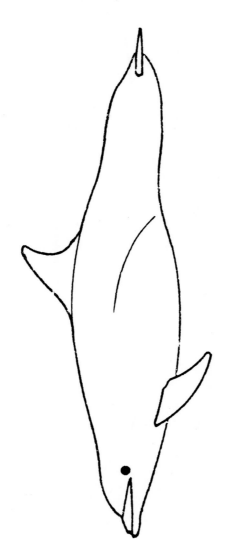

Body Color: Dark grey back, lighter grey sides, white belly.

The bottlenosed porpoise is a popular, well-known mammal because of its use in movies and aquariums. Even in the open ocean they are known to approach humans close enough to be touched. This porpoise is easy to carve and also lends itself well to stylizing.

Poses: Almost any pose works for the porpoise from flat to leaping to tailwalking and more

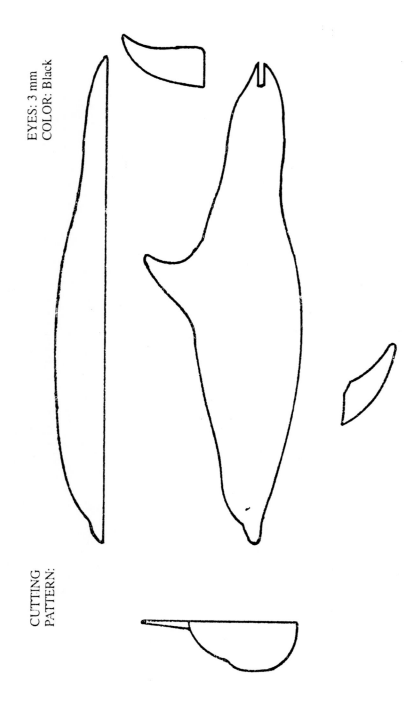

EYES: 3 mm
COLOR: Black

CUTTING
PATTERN:

MAKO SHARK
(Isurus oxyrinchus)

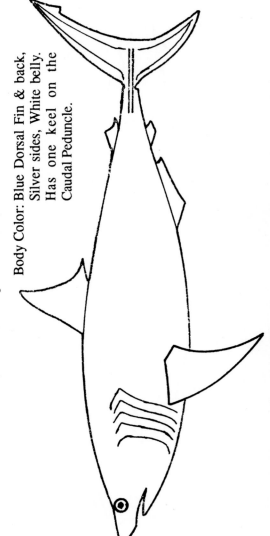

Body Color: Blue Dorsal Fin & back, Silver sides, White belly. Has one keel on the Caudal Peduncle.

The Mako Shark is the fastest shark in the ocean. It feeds on many of the fastest fish such as mackerel, bonito, and tuna. The Mako is 6-12 feet long and weighs up to 1000 pounds. It is also known as the Sharpnose Mako, or the Shortfin Mako. When it is hooked it leaps and fights, making it a desirable sport fish.

Poses: Some good poses for the Mako are leaping, or fighting a fishing line. The Mako also is impressive as a side mount in a shadow box or picture frame.

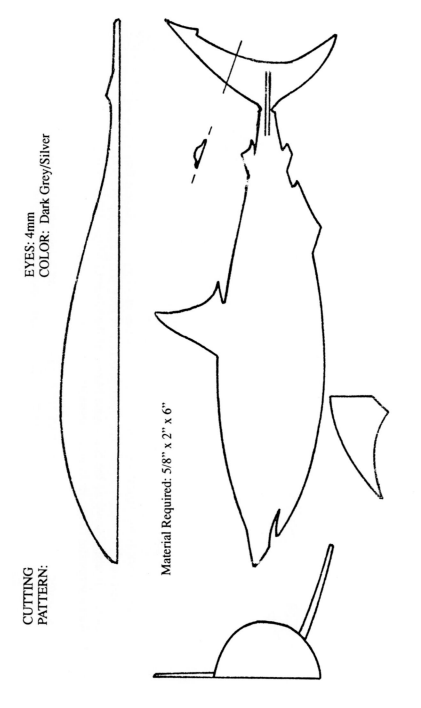

EYES: 4mm
COLOR: Dark Grey/Silver

CUTTING
PATTERN:

Material Required: 5/8" x 2" x 6"

Note: Dorsal fin can be carved separately if desired. Pelvic fin is shown attached and should be carved at a slight angle a small distance (1/64) from Center line.

Carving Fish — Miniature Saltwater and Freshwater

GREAT BLUE SHARK
(Prionace glauca)

Body Color: Blue to lateral line , silver below. Blue anal fins and pectoral.

The great blue shark with its dorsal fin and tail out of the water is a truly memorable sight, but is mostly a fish eater. Its small gill slits, pointed snout, and long pectoral fin make it an impressive and fun fish to carve.

Poses: A tailflip on this shark does not detract from its streamlined shape.

EYES: 3-4 mm
COLOR: Silver/Yellow

CUTTING
PATTERN:

Material Required: 1/2" x 1 1/2" x 7"

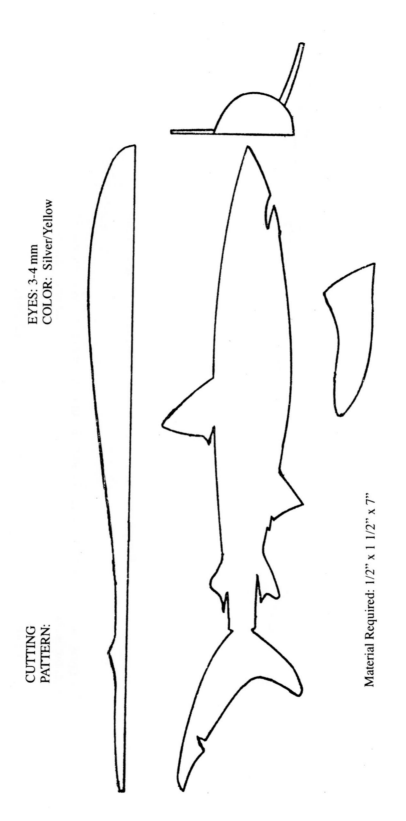

Carving Fish — Miniature Saltwater and Freshwater

THRESHER SHARK
(Alopias vulpinus)

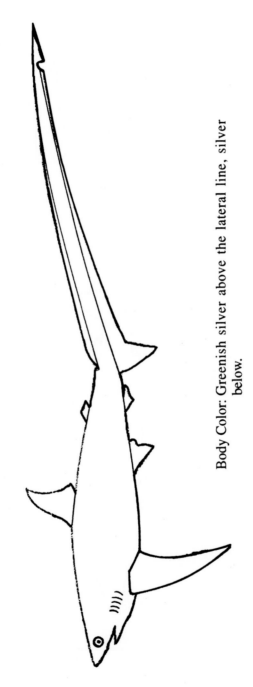

Body Color: Greenish silver above the lateral line, silver below.

The thresher shark at 14 to 18 feet and 500 to 700 pounds is quite a spectacular catch for the recreational fisherman. The upper tail is as long or longer than the body. Carving the thresher is a challenge but is well worth the added care.

Poses: The easiest and most dramatic pose is flat.

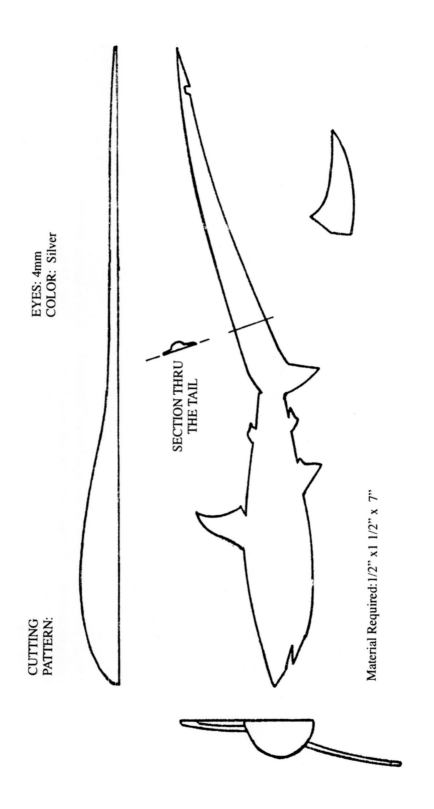

EYES: 4mm
COLOR: Silver

CUTTING
PATTERN:

SECTION THRU
THE TAIL

Material Required: 1/2" x 1 1/2" x 7"

Carving Fish — Miniature Saltwater and Freshwater

SAILFISH
(Istiophorus platypterus)

Body Color: Sides are blue above the lateral line and silver below. The dorsal fin is blue with black spots.

The sailfish is a very popular ocean gamefish in both the Atlantic and Pacific. They combine runs up to 60 miles per hour with leaps and hookshakes for hours of fighting. The sailfish is easy to carve and paint. The pelvic fins can be made out of fine copper wire or they can be left off.

Poses: The Sailfish should be posed with at least a tail flip. A leaping sailfish makes an impressive desk set.

CUTTING
PATTERN:

EYES: 4mm
COLOR: Silver/Blue

Material Required: 1/2" x 2" x 6 1/2" Body
1/16" x 1 1/4" x 3" Dorsal Fin.

Note: The two keels on the caudal peduncle are prominent. The dorsal fin is easier to carve separately and attach last.

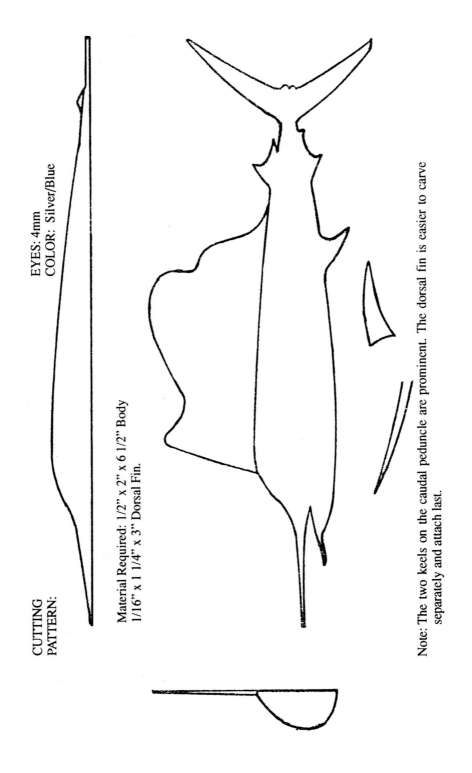

BLUE MARLIN
(Makaira nigricans)

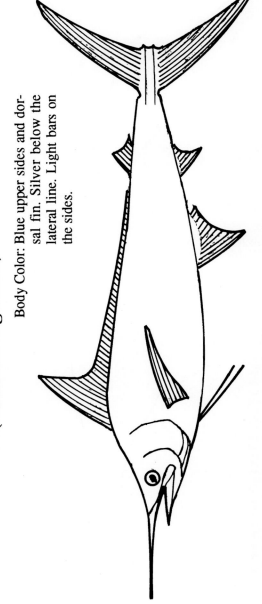

Body Color: Blue upper sides and dorsal fin. Silver below the lateral line. Light bars on the sides.

Weighing in at an average of 75 to 100 pounds, the Blue Marlin is a formidable opponent. When hooked he makes many leaps before tiring. The Marlin's bill should be treated with superglue to keep it from breaking.

Poses: The Marlin can be posed flat or with a tail flip. A leaping pose on a pen set is a good present for a fisherman.

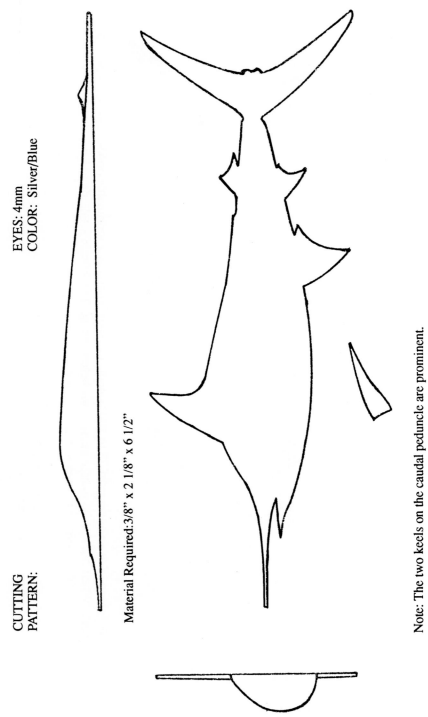

EYES: 4mm
COLOR: Silver/Blue

CUTTING
PATTERN:

Material Required: 3/8" x 2 1/8" x 6 1/2"

Note: The two keels on the caudal peduncle are prominent.

Carving Fish — Miniature Saltwater and Freshwater

BLUEFIN TUNA
(Thunnus thynnus)

Body Color: Blackish-blue back, silver sides and belly. Yellowish anal fins and finlets. Yellow band separates the back and side colors to approximately the anal fin.

The Bluefin Tuna is the largest ot the tunas and is caught mainly as a sportfish. Because of its ability to fight for hours it is a highly sought after fish and has been the subject of many tournaments. The Bluefin Tuna is a fun fish to carve with its bullet shape and finlets.

Poses: A flat pose shows off the streamlined shape very well.

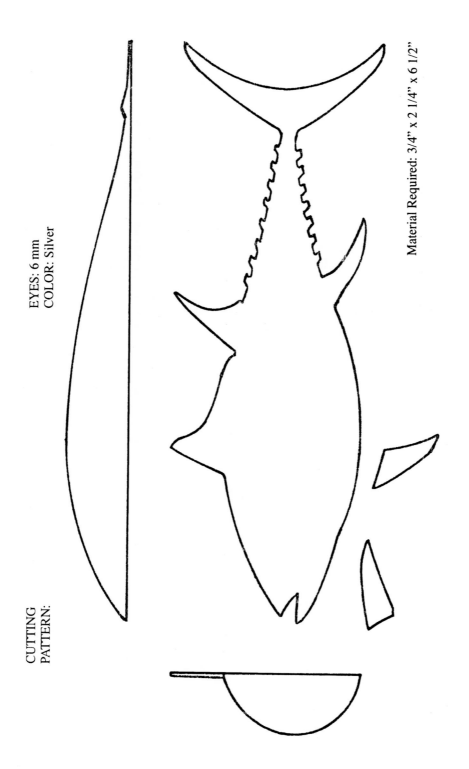

EYES: 6 mm
COLOR: Silver

Material Required: 3/4" x 2 1/4" x 6 1/2"

CUTTING
PATTERN:

Carving Fish — Miniature Saltwater and Freshwater

DOLPHIN
(Coryphaena hippurus)

Body Color: Dorsal fin and back are blue fading into green to the lateral line. Below the lateral line is yellow fading into silver on the belly. There are light and dark spots of various sizes on the sides

The dolphin is a popular saltwater gamefish. Tailwalking and out-of-the-water leaps combined with mad dashes at 50 miles per hour make it one of the hardest fish to keep on the line. The dolphin is an easy fish to carve with its tapering shape from head to tail and sloping back.

Poses: The dolphin looks fast in a flat pose or slight tail flip. A slight body bend on a plaque will still give the illusion of speed.

EYES: 4mm
COLOR: Silver/Yellow

Material Required: 1/2" x 2 3/8" x 7"

CUTTING
PATTERN:

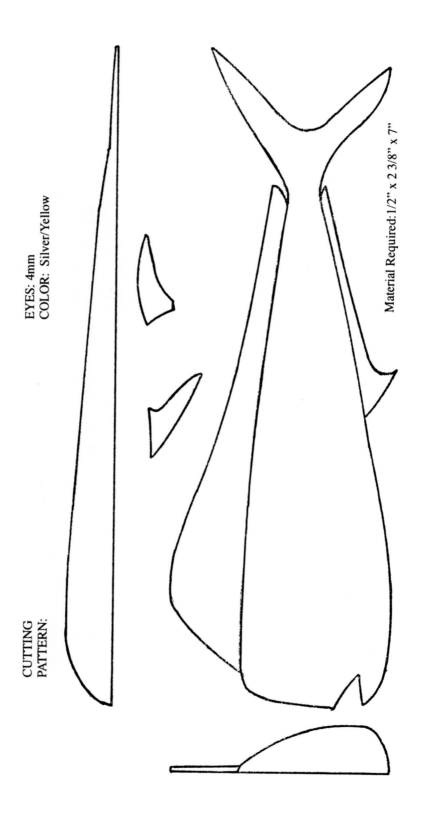

Carving Fish — Miniature Saltwater and Freshwater

SOCKEYE SALMON or KOKANEE
(Oncorhynchus nerka)

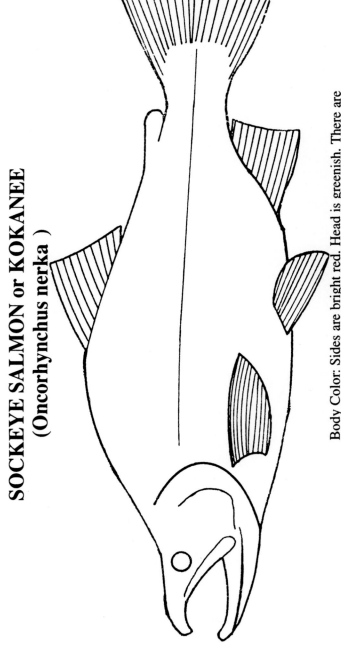

Body Color: Sides are bright red. Head is greenish. There are small black spots on side. White belly.

The Pacific sockeye is a commercial fish, but the kokanee, a landlocked form, has been introduced into the lakes around the West and provides great sport for fishermen. The bright red mating colors and hooked jaw make it a striking fish to carve and paint.

Poses: The kokanee should be posed flat. When done in their mating colors they make impressive wall plaques.

Carving Fish — Miniature Saltwater and Freshwater

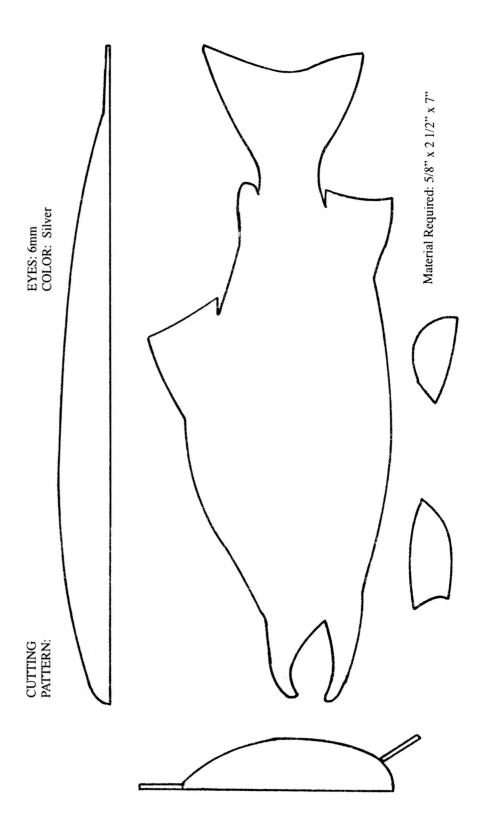

EYES: 6mm
COLOR: Silver

Material Required: 5/8" x 2 1/2" x 7"

CUTTING
PATTERN:

Carving Fish — Miniature Saltwater and Freshwater

COHO SALMON
(Oncorhynchus kisutch)

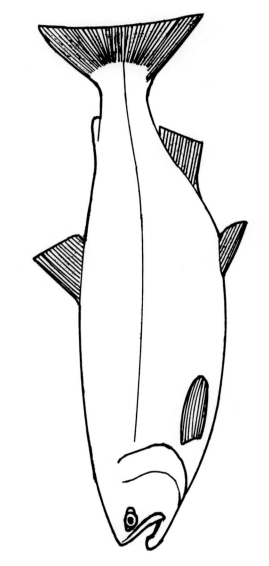

Body Color: Silvery blue sides with spots above the lateral line and on the upper part of the tail.

The coho is native to the Pacific Ocean, but is now also found in the Great Lakes. A great sport fish, it fights near the top of the water and leaps into the air. Average sizes are 5 to 10 pounds and 16 to 20 inches.

Poses: The coho looks good with a tail flip or as a leaping fish on a pen set.

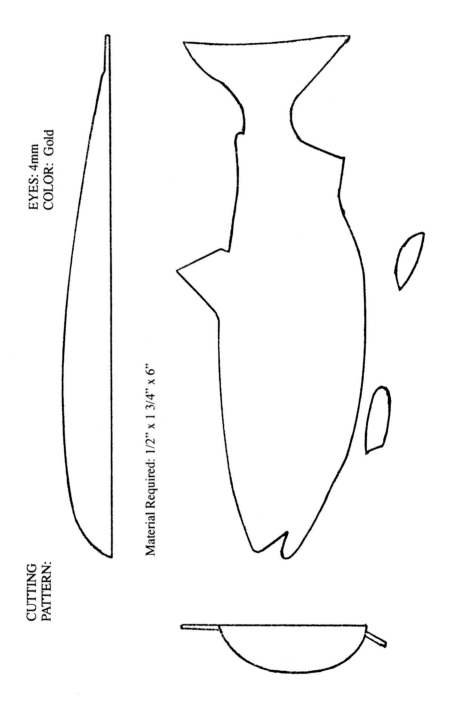

EYES: 4mm
COLOR: Gold

CUTTING
PATTERN:

Material Required: 1/2" x 1 3/4" x 6"

Carving Fish — Miniature Saltwater and Freshwater

PINK SALMON
(Oncorhynchus gorbuscha)

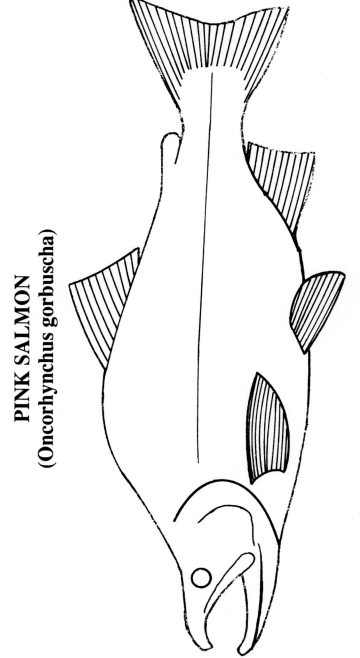

Body Color: Pink sides with black spots. Head silver with a greenish cast. White belly.

The pink salmon is the smallest Pacific salmon, but it is fished for by sports fishermen because it will take lures. The hump is more pronounced than the sockeye so it also is known as the humpback salmon. The pink salmon is a very distinctive fish and is fun to carve.

Poses: The pink salmon can be posed flat or with a slight tailflip.

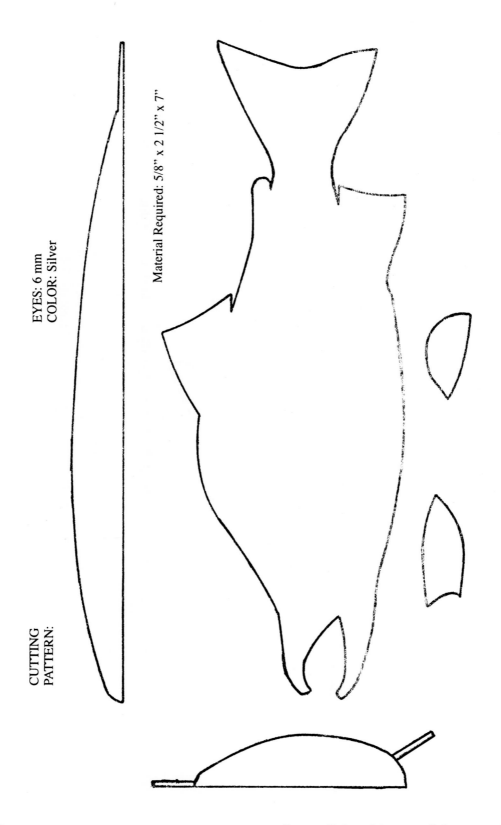

EYES: 6 mm
COLOR: Silver

Material Required: 5/8" x 2 1/2" x 7"

CUTTING
PATTERN:

RAINBOW TROUT
(Salmo gairdneri)

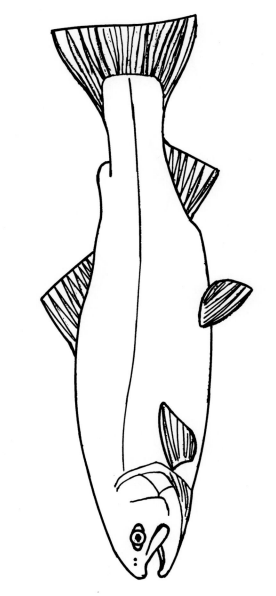

Body Color: Green on upper sides and back and tail. Pink stripe from gill to tail. Random black spots on the sides. White belly.

The rainbow is one of the favorite fly casting sport fishes and is known for its fierce fighting characteristics. A 1 foot to 14" rainbow is a prize catch with its distinctive pink stripe. Some rainbows migrate to the sea, but most stay in cold, clear rivers and streams. The eye pocket on the front and back of the eye and the caudal peduncle extension into the tail fin makes the rainbow an interesting fish to carve.

Poses: The rainbow should have at least a tail flip. A back arch and/or leaping pose would make an impressive pen set.

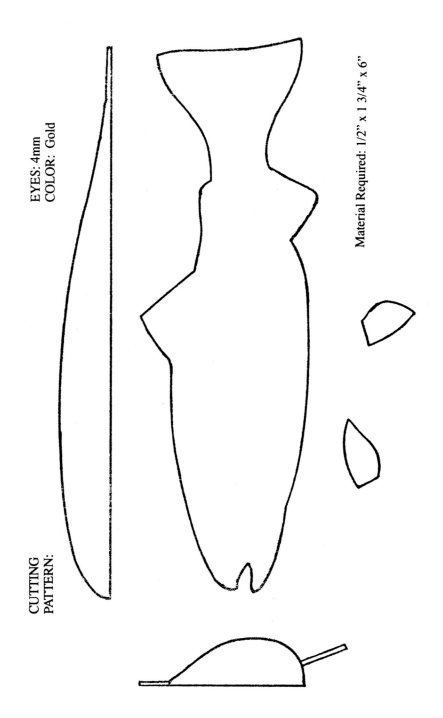

EYES: 4mm
COLOR: Gold

Material Required: 1/2" x 1 3/4" x 6"

CUTTING
PATTERN:

Carving Fish — Miniature Saltwater and Freshwater

QUEEN ANGELFISH
(Holocanthus ciliaris)

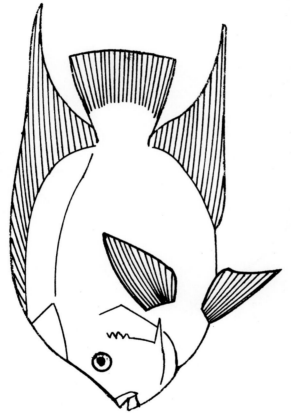

Body Color: Sides are green with yellow highlights, the dorsal and anal fins are yellow with blue edges, the pectoral, pelvic, and caudal fins are yellow. A black eyespot ringed with blue is on the forehead.

The queen angel is native to Florida and is one of the most colorful fishes. They can reach a length of 2 feet and are good eating. The queen angel is fun to paint and carve.

Poses: A small queen angel makes a striking pin. The queen angel looks best posed flat.

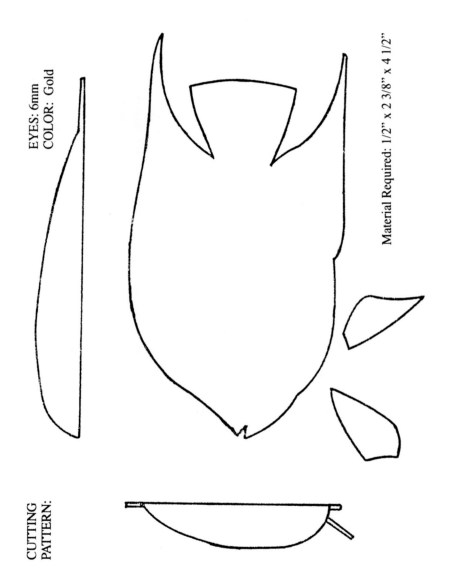

EYES: 6mm
COLOR: Gold

Material Required: 1/2" x 2 3/8" x 4 1/2"

CUTTING
PATTERN:

Carving Fish — Miniature Saltwater and Freshwater

BLACK ANGEL
(Pomacanthus aureus)

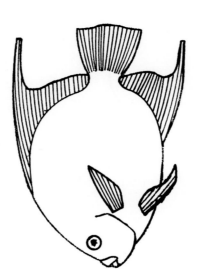

Body Color:Black with a white tail band and white edging on the trailing edges of the fins. White lips.

The black angel is a tropical fish found in many aquariums. The small size and shape and black-and-white coloring make the black angel an easy project to carve. This would be a good fish to practice using a mesh (net or tulle) to make the scales.

Poses: The black angel looks best posed flat or with a slight tail flip.

EYES: 4 mm
COLOR: Gold

CUTTING
PATTERN:

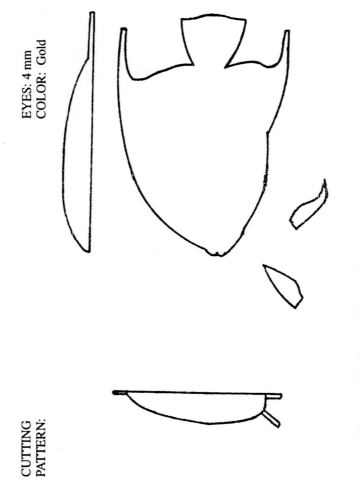

Material Required:5/16" x 1 3/4" x 2 3/4"

COPPERBAND BUTTERFLYFISH
(Chelmon rostratus)

Body Color: White with orange bands.
Black eye spot with white and black edge.
Black edging on the orange bands.

The butterfly fish is a colorful tropical fish from the Indo-Pacific. This fish is fun to carve but its bright orange bands also make it fun to paint.

Poses: A flat pose shows off the butterfly nicely. A slight tail flip, as shown, is probably the most action you would want. A few butterflies in a mock aquarium setting or as a pin are also effective.

EYES: 6mm
COLOR: Gold

Material Required: 3/8" x 2 1/4" x 3 1/4"

CUTTING
PATTERN:

90   Carving Fish — Miniature Saltwater and Freshwater

RED-BELLIED PIRANHA
(Serrasalmus nattereri)

Body Color: Green above the lateral line fading to silvery white below. Red below the middle of the gill cover to the anal fin.

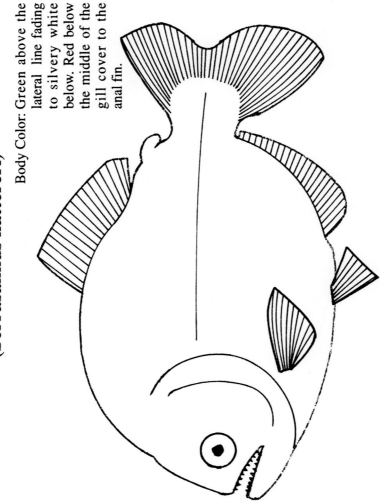

The piranha is known for its voracious eating habits and with its razor-sharp teeth can devour a large animal in minutes. The piranha is no longer permitted in private aquariums so the best way to display them is carved. Don't forget to insert many teeth in your carving.

Poses: Flat with its mouth open and teeth showing is an impressive display.

EYES: 10 mm
COLOR: Red

Material Required: 5/8" x 3 1/4" x 5 1/8"

CUTTING PATTERN:

Carving Fish — Miniature Saltwater and Freshwater

MUSKELLUNGE (MUSKIE)
(Esox masquinongy)

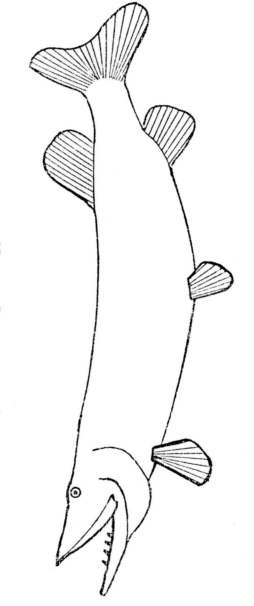

Body Color: Green to brownish sides with markings of vertically oriented darker spots. (Do not line the spots in rows.)

The Muskie is one of the largest game fish of the Upper Midwest. Weighing up to 70 pounds and up to 5 feet long it is a worthy fighter, leaping out of the water in spectacular twisting turning jumps.

Poses: The Muskie can be posed leaping or fighting a fishing line. A shadow box or picture frame sets off the Muskie if a tail flip and open mouth are used. Teeth help make the Muskie look ferocious.

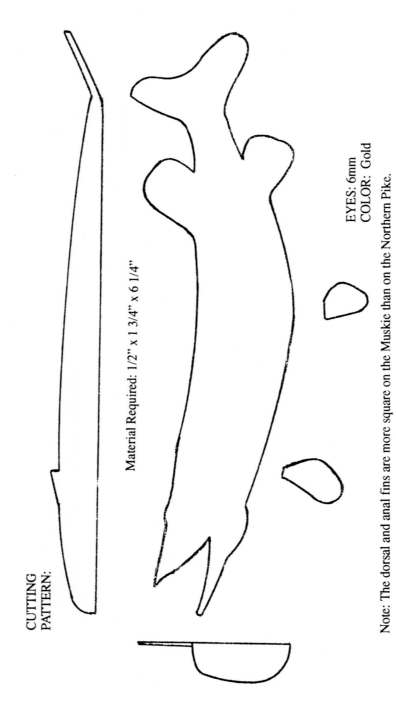

CUTTING
PATTERN:

Material Required: 1/2" x 1 3/4" x 6 1/4"

EYES: 6mm
COLOR: Gold

Note: The dorsal and anal fins are more square on the Muskie than on the Northern Pike.

Carving Fish — Miniature Saltwater and Freshwater

NORTHERN PIKE
(Esox lucius)

Body Color: Dark greenish to green-brown with light green or yellow-green oval spots along the body, the spots tend to be in horizontal rows. White belly and darker green on the back.

The Northern Pike is a worthy adversary for the sport fisherman. A 10-pound Northern is not uncommon and when hooked will either leap out of the water or head for the weeds or bottom to try to break the line. Many of the non-trophy catches end up on the dinner table.

Poses: The Northern can be posed leaping and makes an impressive desk set mount, if done full body. The northern looks best when the mouth is open and the teeth are displayed.

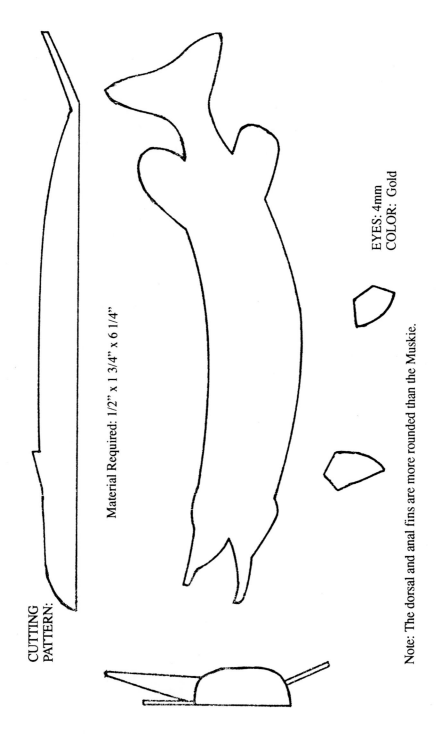

CUTTING PATTERN:

Material Required: 1/2" x 1 3/4" x 6 1/4"

EYES: 4mm
COLOR: Gold

Note: The dorsal and anal fins are more rounded than the Muskie.

Carving Fish — Miniature Saltwater and Freshwater

WALLEYE
(Stizostedion vitreum)

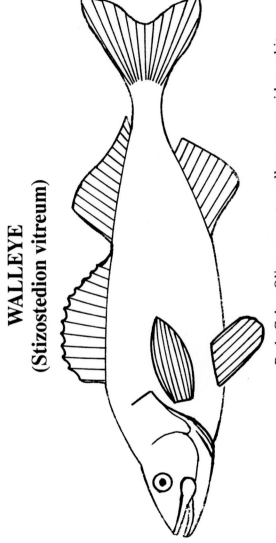

Body Color: Olive green to yellow green sides, white belly. Black blotches on upper sides. Black blotch on last rays of front dorsal fin.

The walleye is the largest fish in the perch family. Many walleyes are caught at night which makes their large eyes more prominent because they glow like a cat's eyes. Walleyes are a good eating fish as well as a worthy adversary.

Poses: Walleyes look good with a tail flip or flat. If done with the mouth open, more than the shown teeth should be added. Minimum gill flare looks the best.

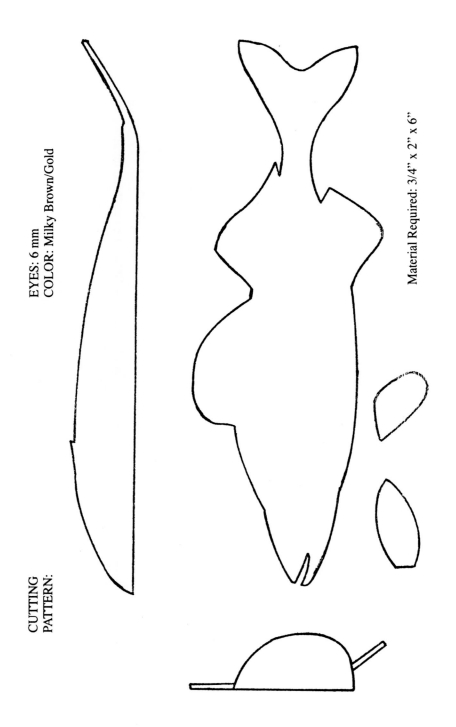

EYES: 6 mm
COLOR: Milky Brown/Gold

Material Required: 3/4" x 2" x 6"

CUTTING
PATTERN:

Carving Fish — Miniature Saltwater and Freshwater

YELLOW PERCH
(PERCA FLAVENCENS)

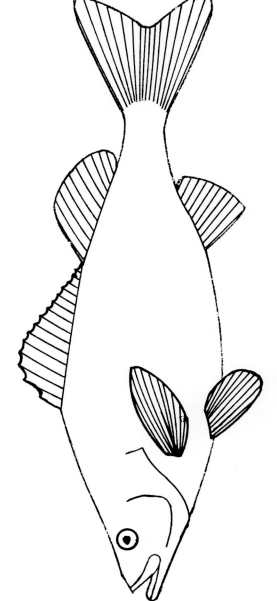

Body Color: Yellow sides with white belly. Black bars on sides fading out toward belly.

The Yellow Perch is a delicious panfish that travels in small schools. Many fishermen have fond memories of catching their first perch with grandpa. The gill corner ends in a sharp point and the head is concave over the eyes. There are seven black bars on the body.

Poses: The best post is a flat pose, but a tail flip will add some action. Groupings of two or three make an impressive diorama.

EYES: 6mm
COLOR: Brown/Gold

Material Required: 1/2" x 2 1/2" x 6 1/2"

CUTTING
PATTERN:

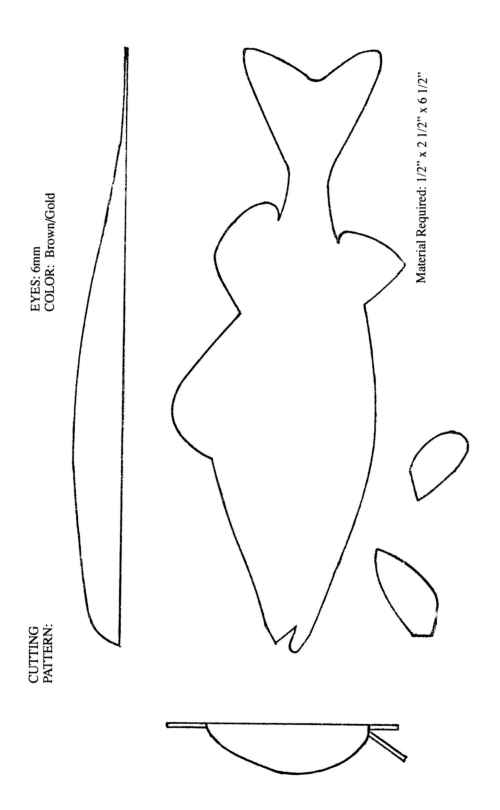

Carving Fish — Miniature Saltwater and Freshwater

BLACK CRAPPIE
(Pomoxis nigromaculatus)

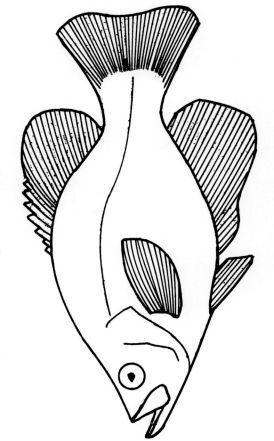

Body Color: Silver-green to greenish sides with black spots in an irregular pattern. White belly.

The Black Crappie is one of the best tasting panfish, and is highly sought after by many anglers. Crappies school, so if one is caught there are more waiting to be caught. Crappies like to hide around fallen logs or branches, which challenges the angler. The Crappie is an easy fish to carve.

Poses: The Crappie looks good flat or with a slight tail flip. Smaller crappie versions can be used as a pin or hat ornament.

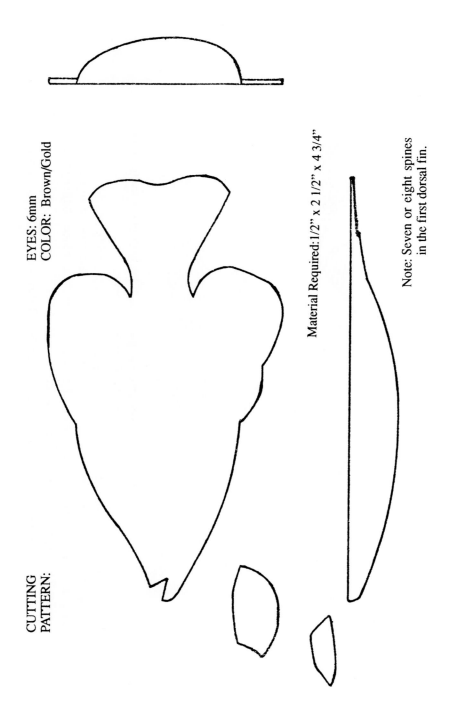

EYES: 6mm
COLOR: Brown/Gold

CUTTING
PATTERN:

Material Required:1/2" x 2 1/2" x 4 3/4"

Note: Seven or eight spines
in the first dorsal fin.

BLUEGILL
(Lepomis macrochirus)

Body Color: Sides are greenish-blue with darker brown vertical bars. Dark blue spots on the soft dorsal fin and ear flap. Looks best with a red belly.

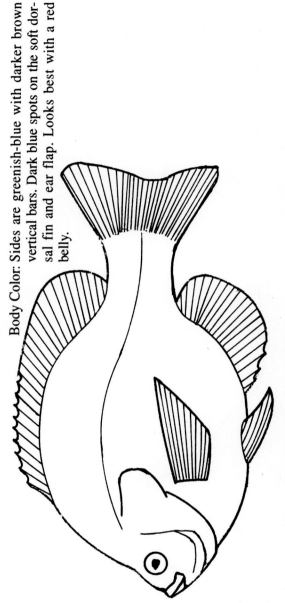

Bluegills are the light tackle fisherman's delight and will bite on almost any bait. Their small mouths require small hooks but they are hard fighters and a good catch of them makes a tasty meal. The males have a bright red belly during the mating season.

Poses: Pose bluegills flat or with a slight tail flip. Bluegills look good in a picture frame.

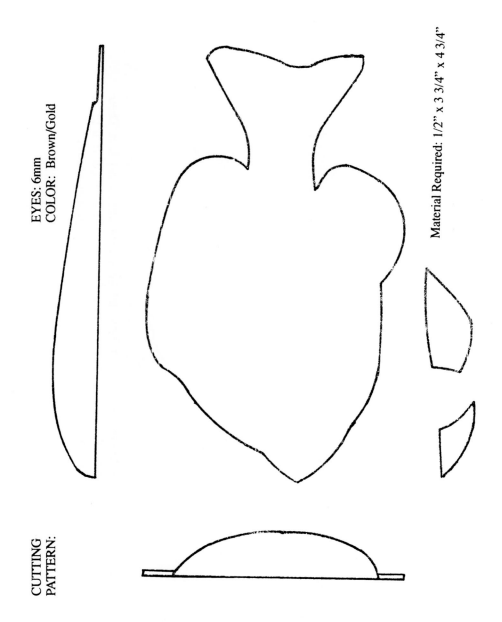

EYES: 6mm
COLOR: Brown/Gold

Material Required: 1/2" x 3 3/4" x 4 3/4"

CUTTING
PATTERN:

SUNFISH or PUMPKINSEED
(Lepomis gibbosus)

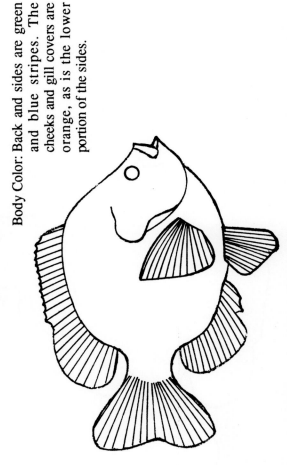

Body Color: Back and sides are green and blue stripes. The cheeks and gill covers are orange, as is the lower portion of the sides.

Sunfish sizes range from 4 to 6 inches, but their size does not diminish the fun of catching them with light tackle. Many fishermen started their hobby, fishing for sunnies.

Poses: Sunnies look best flat. A few sunfish in a shadow box is a stunning eyecatcher. Sunfish make nice pins with their bright orange setting off many outfits.

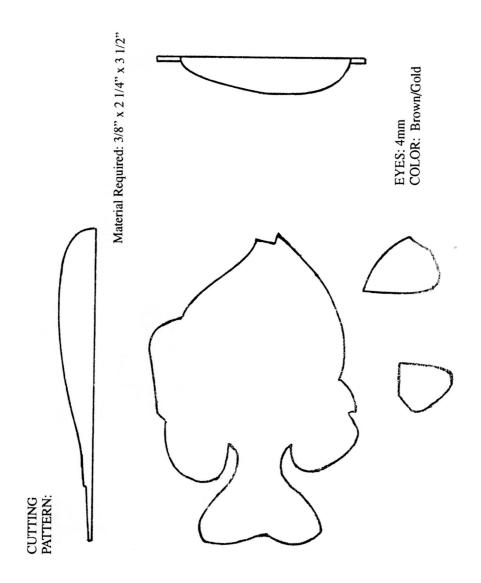

Material Required: 3/8" x 2 1/4" x 3 1/2"

EYES: 4mm
COLOR: Brown/Gold

CUTTING
PATTERN:

Carving Fish — Miniature Saltwater and Freshwater

LARGEMOUTH BLACK BASS
(Microterus salmoides)

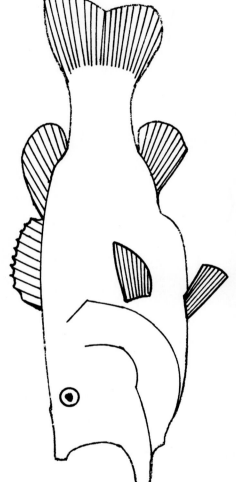

Body Color: Blackish-green above the lateral line, yellowish-green below. Vertical black bars at the lateral line. White belly.

The largemouth bass is one of the most sought after freshwater fish in the USA. Fishing clubs, national organizations, special boats, and a host of special equipment are available for the bass fisherman. It is only appropriate that a carved bass be a spectacular display, even though it may be a bit harder to carve with its mouth gaping and its gills flaring.

Poses: A wide-open mouth and gills with a tail flip is the least amount of action a bass should have.

EYES: 6 mm
COLOR: Brown/Gold

Material Required: 1" x 1 7/8" x 5 3/8"

CUTTING
PATTERN:

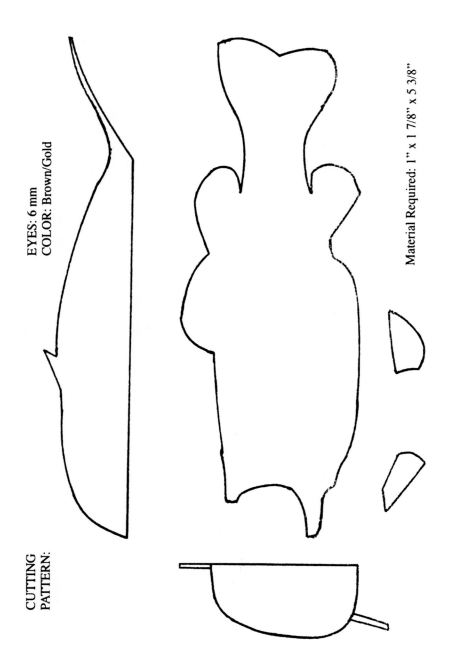

Stylized
Porpoise

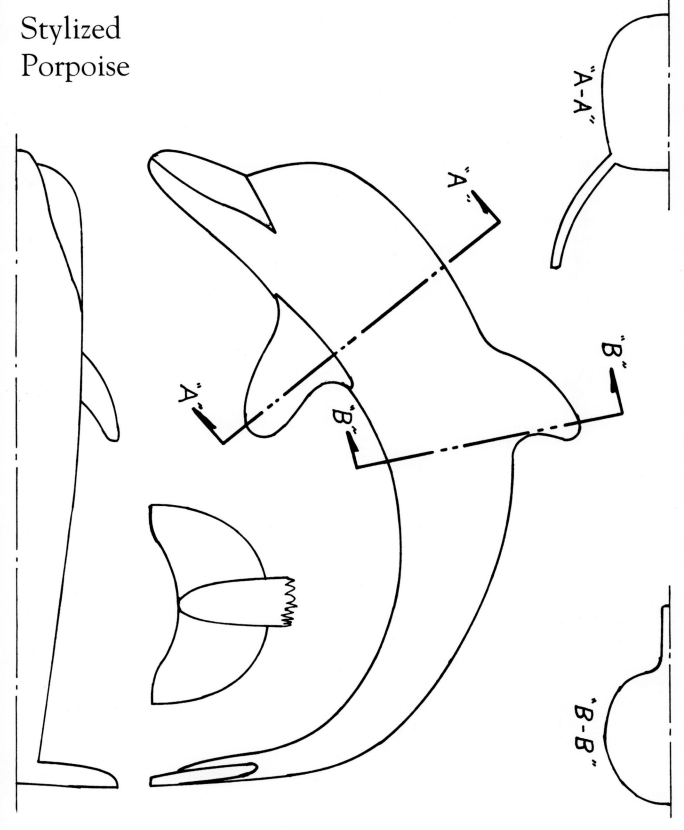

"A-A"

"A"

"A"

"B"

"B"

"B-B"

Index

You are invited to Join the

National Wood Carvers Association

"Some carve their careers: others just chisel"

since 1953

If you have any interest in woodcarving: if you carve wood, create wood sculpture or even just whittle in your spare time, you will enjoy your membership in the National Wood Carvers Association. The non-profit NWCA is the world's largest carving club with over 33,000 members. There are NWCA members in more than 56 countries around the globe.

The Association's goals are to:

- promote wood carving
- foster fellowship among member enthusiasts
- encourage exhibitions and area get togethers
- list sources of equipment and information for the wood carving artist
- provide a forum for carving artists

The NWCA serves as a valuable network of tips, hints and helpful information for the wood carver. Membership is only $11.00 per year.

Members receive the magazine "Chip Chats" six times a year, free with their membership. "Chip Chats" contains articles, news events, demonstrations of technique, patterns and a full color section showcasing examples of fine craftsmanship. Through this magazine you will be kept up to date on shows and workshops to attend, new products, special offers to NWCA members and other members' activities in your area and around the world.

National Wood Carvers Association

7424 Miami Ave.
Cincinnati, OH 45243

Name: _____

Address:_____

_____

Dues $11.00 per year in USA, $14.00 per year foreign (payable in US Funds)

Fox Chapel Publishing

How-To and Reference Books from the Experts

Woodworking Titles

Easy to Make Wooden Inlay Projects: Intarsia
New second edition. Full color project gallery. Includes 12 ready to use patterns.
Intarsia is a method of making picture mosaics in wood, using a combination of wood grains and colors. The techniques and step-by-step instructions in this book will have you completing your own beautiful pieces in short order. Written by acknowledged expert Judy Gale Roberts, who has her own studio and publishes the Intarsia Times newsletter, produces videos, gives seminars and writes articles on the Intarsia method. Each project is featured in full color and this well written, heavily illustrated features over 100 photographs and includes index and directory of suppliers
    ISBN# 56523-023-X   160 pages, soft cover, 8.5 x 11 inches $19.95

Making Collector Plates on Your Scroll Saw
by Judy Gale Roberts
Hot new title from Judy Gale Roberts (best-selling author of Easy to Make Inlay Wood Projects-INTARSIA). Make personalized commemorative plates for birthdays, weddings anniversaries and other special events.. Easy to follow techniques to make and finish 10 ready to use patterns. Full color on every page. 40+ color photos
soft cover, full color, 64 pages
    ISBN # 1-56523-050-7 $12.95 retail

More great scroll saw books by Judy Gale Roberts!
Fine Line Designs Scroll Saw Fretwork Patterns

Especially designed for the scroll saw enthusiast who wishes to excel, the 'fine line design' method helps you to control drift error found with thick line patterns. Each book features great designs, expert tips, and patterns on oversized (up to 11" x 17" !) sheets in a special "lay flat" spiral binding. Choose the original Design Book 1 with animal and fun designs, or Design Book Two featuring "Western- Southwestern" designs.
    Scroll Saw Fretwork Pattern, Design Book One "The Original" $14.95
    Scroll Saw Fretwork Patterns, Design Book Two "Western-Southwestern" $16.95

Scroll Saw Fretwork Patterns, Design Book Three
    " The Great Outdoors" Patterns for a variety of wildlife, hunting and fishing scenes. $14.95

Scroll Saw Fretwork Patterns, Design Book Four
    "Sports". Patterns for almost every type of sport activity - baseball, football, basketball ... and more.
    $14.95

Scroll Saw Fretwork Patterns, Design Book Five
    "Heartland- Farm & Country". Great country woodworking designs and scenes. $14.95

Scroll Saw Fretwork Patterns, Design Book Six
    " Pets & People" Creative patterns for dog, cat and pet-lovers. $14.95

Scroll Saw Woodcrafting Magic! Complete Pattern and How-to Manual (2nd revised printing)
Includes complete patterns drawn to scale. You will be amazed at how easy it is to make these beautiful projects when you follow Joanne's helpful tips and work from these clear, precise patterns. Never-before-published patterns for original and creative toys, jewelry, and gifts. Never used a scroll saw? The tutorials in this book will get you started quickly. Experienced scroll-sawyers will delight in these all-new, unique projects, perfect for craft sales and gift-giving. Written by Joanne Lockwood, owner of Three Bears Studio in California and the president of the Sacramento Area Woodworkers; she is frequently featured in national woodwork and craft magazines.

    ISBN# 1-56523-024-8   300 pages, soft cover, 8.5 x 11 inches $16.95

The Mott Miniature Furniture Workshop Manual
by Barbara and Elizabeth Mott
THE book for miniature furniture hobbyists. Jam-packed with techniques and patterns. Contains ready to use detailed patterns for 144 projects- from windsor chairs to rocking horses-all to scale. Information on miniature chair caning, wood bending, assembly instructions carving techniques. Over 100 ready to use miniature prints, photos and decals included.
Soft cover, 220 pages
    ISBN# 1-56523-052-3 $19.95 retail

Woodcarving Titles

Woodcarvers Workbook - Carving Animals with Mary Duke Guldan
" Best Woodcarving pattern book I've seen in my 40 years as a carver"
Ed Gallenstein, President National Woodcarvers Association
These complete step-by-step instructionas and easy to follow patterns will guide you through the process of creating beautiful handcarved masterpieces of your own. Woodcarvers Workbook is chock-full ofinteresting notes, expert tips and solid information. Twelve patterns included for moose, bear, dog, wild horses, cougar, rabbits and more. Painting and finishing section.
    1-56523-033-7   softcover 96 pages $14.95

Second Woodcarvers Workbook
by Mary Duke Guldan
Long-awaited second book by acclaimed woodcarving author and National Woodcarving Association columnist. Easy to follow instructions accompany the best carving patterns available any where. Patterns include:
Native Indian Chief, wild animals, farm animals, Texas Longhorn 12 + patterns in all.
Soft cover 96 pages
    ISBN # 1-56523-037-X $14.95 retail

The Fantastic Book of Canes, Pipes and Walking Sticks
by Harry Ameredes
Veteran carver Ameredes has included hundreds of original designs from 35 years of his work in his exciting sketchbook for woodcarvers and cane collectors. Includes plans for using driftwood and tree roots to make fabulous one-of-a-kind carvings.
Soft cover 128 pages
ISBN # 1-56523-048-5 $12.95 retail

Woodcarving Adventure Movie Caricatures
with Jim Maxwell
Jim Maxwell turns his creative eye to carving caricatures of our favorite movie stars. Create your own striking carvings of John Wayne, Indiana Jones and others. Heavily illustrated with over 225 photos of step-by-step instructions and finished projects. Sure to appeal to both beginning and advanced carvers. 12 ready to use patterns included
Soft cover, 128 pages
    ISBN # 1-56523-051-5 $12.95 retail

Making Collectible Santas and Christmas Ornametns in Wood

by Jim and margie Maxwell

These 42 easy to follow projects ill make you very popular this Christmas! Full size patterns included for a Snowman, 10 different Santas, Nutcracker ornament and more. 48 pages.

    Order #Maxwell1 $6.95

Carving Characters with Jim Maxwell

Want to learn how to carve folk characters in wood? This book shows you how from start to finish. In step-by-step photos and instructions, Jim makes it easy. Twelve different project patterns included.

    Order #Maxwell2 $6.95

Carving Decorative Fish by Jim Jensen

26 detailed patterns for favorite fresh and salt water fish projects accompany an excellent step-by-step technique and photo section that leaves nothing to guess work. Painting how-to section in full color.

Soft cover, 128 pages, b/w and color photos

    ISBN # 1-56523-053-1 $14.95 retail

Mammals: An Artistic Approach by Desiree Hajny

Your chance to learn from one of the world's top notch carvers. Features a helpful step-by-step photo session as Desiree carves an otter. Learn the carving, texturing and painting techniques that have brought worldwide recognition of her work. Patterns anatomy studies and reference photos are inside for deer, bears, otters and more. Color section PLUS a gallery section showing some of her outstanding pieces over the years. Heavily illustrated   Softcover, 180 pages.

    Available NOW   ISBN # 1-56523-036-1 $19.95 retail

Carving Wooden Critters

Includes power carving techniques by Diane Ernst

Diane Ernst's first pattern treasury. A frequent award winner for her cute puppies, rabbits and other critters, Diane's patterns feature multiple views-top, side, front and back and also include wood burning details. A step by step photo session using power carving tools is also included. Buy this book and start carving your own character-filled critters.

    Available NOW   ISBN # 1-56523-038-8 $6.95 retail

Carving Kids with Ivan Whillock

Brand new title from the author of pictorial Relief Carving, and Carving the Head in Wood. Master carver Whillock now turns his talents to carving an engaging series of children's portraits at play - playing baseball, dressing up in Mommy's clothes - ten different projects. Carving techniques are illustrated step-by-step, PLUS complete patterns are included. Full color project gallery. Over 100 illustrations.

    Available NOW   ISBN# 1-56523-045-0 $12.95 retail

Cowtown Carving-by Steve Prescott

Texas Whittling Champion Steve Prescott's collection of 15 original caricature projects features full size plans and excellent instructions for carving and finishing.

Soft cover, 96 pages $14.95

    ISBN # 1-56523-049-3   Available NOW

Woodcarving Books by George Lehman

Learn new techniques as you carve these projects designed by professional artists and carver George Lehman. These best-selling books by a master carver are invaluable reference books, PLUS each book contains over 20 ready-to-use patterns.

Book One - Carving Realistic Game and Songbirds - Patterns and instructions

Enthusiastically received by carvers across the US and Canada. George pays particular attention to the needs of beginning carvers in this volume. 20 patterns, over 70 photos, sketches and reference drawing.

ISBN# 1-56523-004-3   96 pages, spiral bound, 14 x 11 inches, includes index, resources $19.95

Book Two - Realism in Wood - 22 projects, detailed patterns and instructions

This volume features a selection of patterns for shorebirds and birds of prey in addition to all-new duck and songbird patterns. Special sections on adding detail, burning.

ISBN# 1-56523-005-1,   112 pages, spiral bound, 14 x 11 inches, includes index, resources $19.95

Book Three - Nature in Wood - patterns for carving 21 smaller birds and 8 wild animals

Focuses on songbirds and small game birds . Numerous tips and techniques throughout including instruction on necessary skills for creating downy feather details and realistic wings. Wonderful section on wild animal carvings with measured patterns.

ISBN #1-56523-006-X   128 pages, soft bound, 11 x 8.5 inches, includes index, resources $16.95

Book Four - Carving Wildlife in Wood- 20 Exciting Projects

Here is George's newest book for decorative woodcarvers with never-before-published patterns. Tremendously detailed, these patterns appeal to carvers at all skill levels. Patterns for birds of prey, ducks, wild turkey, shorebirds and more! Great addition to any carvers library - will be used again and again.

ISBN #1-56523-007-8   96 pages, spiral-bound, 14 x 11 $19.95

Encyclopedia of Bird Reference Drawings

by David Mohrhardt

This helpful reference features detailed sketches and wing studies for more than 215 different birds. Includes lots of hard-to-find information. Mohrhardt is an award-winning artist. This book contains much material that he gathered for use in his own work. We recommend this book as an excellent general reference for all carvers, bird lovers and artists. Recommended by Bob Guge, World Champion Carver.

ISBN #1-56523-009-4   96 pages $14.95

To order, please send check or money order for price listed plus $2.50 per book postage.

Send to:
Fox Chapel Book Orders
Box 7948B
Lancaster, PA 17604

1(800) 457-9112
Fax (717) 560-4702

Please try your favorite book supplier first!